WORKING WITH CHILDREN AND ANIMALS

WORKING WITH CHILDREN AND ANIMALS

LIZA GODDARD

WITH DEREK CLEMENTS

FOREWORD BY SUSAN JAMESON

APEX PUBLISHING LTD

First published in 2011 by

Apex Publishing Ltd

PO Box 7086, Clacton on Sea, Essex, CO15 5WN

www.apexpublishing.co.uk

British Library Cataloguing-in-Publication Data
A catalogue record for this book
is available from the British Library

ISBN 1-906358-89-3
978-1-906358-89-1

Typeset in 10pt Baskerville Win95BT

Production Manager: Chris Cowlin

Cover photos: Francis Loney

Printed and bound by
MPG Books Group in the UK

Publishers Note:
The views and opinions expressed in this publication are those of the
author and are not necessarily those of Apex Publishing Ltd

Copyright:
Every attempt has been made to contact the relevant copyright holders,
Apex Publishing Ltd would be grateful if the appropriate people contact us on:
01255 428500 or mail@apexpublishing.co.uk

I dedicate this book to Adelaide and Oscar, with all my love

CONTENTS

FOREWORD

Liza Goddard is one of my best mates. And, looking back, that seems to have given her the right to do what lots of people do to mates – drop me in it on a regular basis!

She's found dogs that apparently 'only I can save', she's rescued ponies with problems and palmed them off on me, she's dragged me off to do weird shows in far-flung places at ungodly hours, she's co-opted me onto charity committees and only told me afterwards – and now she's asked me to write this foreword!

Could this be her first serious error in our 35-year friendship? Maybe she thought I'd say a lot of typical luvvy things about her? About how gorgeous she is, how brilliant, how tough, how talented? Perhaps she thought I'd harp on about her boundless energy, and her irritatingly youthful appearance? (She must have a picture in the attic). Maybe I'd add that she's funny, and kind, a loyal friend, a bit of an intellectual and a word puzzle champion?

She gave me the chance to say all that, but why on earth should I?

Just cos it's true there's no need to go on about it.

She'll probably do all that in this book. Enjoy!

Susan Jameson

PROLOGUE
IN THE BEGINNING

"I keep thinking that I will wake up one day and find it has all been a dream."

For as long as I can remember, all that I ever wanted to do was act.

It may have had something to do with the fact that I made my stage debut at Farnham Rep at the age of 18 months, as the infant Queen Elizabeth in *The Merry Wives of Windsor*. This, of course, was a performance that I knew nothing about. Or it could be because I was thrown into the limelight by my father, who worked for the BBC, when the director of one series he was working on was looking for children – Dad said that he had two daughters. My sister hated it, I loved it, and so a dream was born, and from that moment I knew it was what I wanted to do with my life.

I spent every waking moment dreaming of being on stage, and was always the first one to volunteer for school plays and musicals. Then, after pestering my parents non-stop, I was sent to drama school, where I studied with the likes of Nigel Havers, Susie Blake and Jane Seymour.

Since those days, I have been fortunate enough to work with some great classical, film, TV and comedy actors – the likes of Richard Burton, Laurence Olivier, John Gielgud, Kenneth More, Joan Plowright,

Vanessa Redgrave, Coral Browne, Dick Emery, David Jason, Nigel Planer, Susan Jameson, James Bolam, George Cole, Dennis Waterman, Robert Powell, John Nettles, Jimmy Edwards and Julian Fellowes.

I have appeared in some of Britain's most iconic TV series, including *The Brothers*, *Take Three Girls* and *Dr Who*. And, for a while, I even had my own little series on television – what a thrill that was. For reasons that I have never quite been able to fathom, much of my career has involved children's programmes, and I have loved every single moment of that too.

I even thought for a brief moment back there that I might be on the brink of making the big time in America. The salary they were talking about was like listening to somebody reel off their telephone number. It didn't work out in the end, but I have absolutely no regrets, especially when I see just how neurotic some so-called American stars are – that could have been me. It really could.

Then there was pantomime. Have you any idea how much hard work is involved, and how exhausting it all is? And have you any idea what a sheer joy it is to do? To see the faces of hundreds of young children light up or laugh at a corny joke makes it all worthwhile. Gloriously so.

I have been married to former Dr Who Colin Baker and to 1970s' pop superstar Alvin Stardust, and I have two wonderful children, Thom and Sophie. And, eventually, I found the right man in David Cobham, who has been by my side through some pretty traumatic times.

More recently, my life has been dominated by Alan Ayckbourn, Britain's greatest living playwright, and perhaps the best there has ever been. I really don't know what I did to win his favour, but it would appear that he has a soft spot for me, and he tells me that I am a better actress than I believe I am.

There have been some dark days too – none more so than when I was diagnosed with breast cancer and was told that both my breasts would have to be removed. It was a tough time, but I battled through it all and came out the other side. My beloved husband has also fought his own health battles, but he, too, remains to tell the tale, and one of the best things about it all was that I got to work with him on several shows.

Like everybody else, I have made mistakes and I have regrets but, on the whole, I have had a very rewarding adventure, and one of the most important lessons I have learnt is that we must all live every day of our lives to the full, and try to enjoy it because you never know what is around the corner.

I have been blessed in so many ways, working almost non-stop throughout my career. I keep thinking that I will wake up one day and find it has all been a dream, or that somebody will find me out, and I will never work again. But, so far, it hasn't happened.

And do you know what? I owe it all to a kangaroo.

They say that you should never work with children and animals, but I seem to have spent my entire career doing precisely that. It all started with a kangaroo called Skippy. Or, more accurately, it all started with a whole host of kangaroos, none of which were actually called Skippy.

So how does a young English girl end up being cast in what became arguably the most popular Australian TV series of all time? Yes, I know that there might be some of you who will point to *Neighbours*, but I stand my ground, notwithstanding the fact that *Neighbours* gave us the likes of Jason Donovan and Kylie Minogue.

Skippy put kangaroos on the map! And me too...

www.apexpublishing.co.uk

CHAPTER 1
FINDING MY FEET

"This is for me. This is what I want to do. I want to become an actress like Hayley Mills."

I was born in Smethwick on 20 January, 1950, in the same nursing home as Julie Walters. My mother, Claire Frances Wyton, came from Smethwick. She would deny it but then again, she suffers from dementia and would deny most things. My father was David Michael Goddard.

My parents married six months after I was born in 1950. Nobody would bat an eyelid about such a thing now but I am guessing that a few eyebrows were raised back then because it was generally frowned upon to have a child out of wedlock. I should also perhaps explain that David may not actually have been my father.

Mother, who was an only child, was a very colourful character. Her father died when she was still quite young, having worked for Shell, while her grandfather owned a bicycle shop.

My mother had been married previously and at the end of the Second World War she met, fell in love with and ran away with a Russian prince called Nikolai Obolensky. He was a famous sportsman who was especially well known as a skier. He also played rugby union.

That all ended in tears, and thus she ended up meeting David. I came along seven months after they first got together, so you can draw your own conclusions. Either I was two months early, which is what I was told, or my father was a prince.

In any event, I never met him and grew up regarding David Goddard as my father. His family, who came from Burton on Trent, owned a number of clothing shops and were very wealthy, although my grandfather was a science master at Winchester College. My earliest memories of my grandparents are of staying in a massive schoolhouse – my grandfather, who fought in the First World War, had a private income of £7,000 a year, which was a fortune in those days.

I remember that everywhere I looked at Winchester there were boys, which was hardly surprising since it was a boys' school. There was also a most wonderful cook called Ethel who used to produce fabulous meals. I used to stand at the railings and look down into the kitchen and watch her at work and catch all the wonderful aromas that used to gently float through the air. It was blissful.

My father, who had two brothers and a sister, ended up going to Winchester. I often wondered what it must have been like for him to have attended the school, knowing that his own father was one of the teachers.

Dad had fought in the Second World War, serving with the Rifle Brigade, and he had been awarded the MC – it was something that he never talked about, although he used to joke that he received it following hand-to-hand combat in the Ruhr Valley. He actually received the Military Cross for getting his platoon safely across a minefield. Nowadays, such an act of bravery would be plastered all over the papers but back then these men truly were unsung heroes, interested only in serving their country, seeing off the threat from Hitler and the Nazis and then getting back home to their families. In one piece if they were very lucky.

It is difficult to conceive of it now, but at the age of 20 he was a captain and, for a time, an acting major because the platoon's major had been killed. Father used to say that his survival, and that of all his men, was down to his sergeant-major. "I wouldn't do that if I were you, sir," he used to say, and would then proceed to announce precisely what he would do. My father knew better than to ignore this man, and so that is how he survived the war and then he met my mother.

Not everybody was so lucky. One of his brothers did not make it home, being killed when his motor torpedo boat was sunk, and his other brother became a tea planter in Ceylon. His sister emigrated to New Zealand. She was an amazing woman who had played amateur golf for Cornwall.

Granny was a pianist and her sister played the violin. During the war the pair of them used to play for injured soldiers. As if it wasn't bad enough that they had suffered some kind of injury, the poor chaps then had to sit there and listen to this music, whether they liked it or not. My granny was a wonderful woman.

My father had studied the classics at Winchester and went on to attend Oxford University and at the end of the war he ended up assisting with the defence of a number of minor war criminals at the Nuremburg Trials. He wasn't a barrister, but he was given no say in the matter. He hated every minute of it, which is no surprise really since he had helped to liberate a concentration camp. How can you defend the indefensible? Some of the evidence he heard had a deep impact upon him, just as it would on anybody. But these men had to have representation.

He then moved to the Greek island of Rhodes, where he became a public prosecutor. He spoke Greek, but always said that everybody understood him because the language he was using was actually ancient Greek. Years later I read *Captain Corelli's Mandolin* by Louis de Bernieres and there was a character in the book who also only spoke ancient Greek. I never did work out whether my father was pulling my leg.

One thing I do know, however, is that at one point Dad was in a plane flying home from Cairo when he suffered a mastoid. Nowadays it is nothing, but back then it was a big deal and could have killed him. Fortunately, there was a surgeon on the plane and he operated on my father and saved his life.

One of his jobs as public prosecutor was to stamp the cards of the island's prostitutes. They had to have a medical on a regular basis to prove that they were clean, and Dad would stamp a card which the girls could show to potential clients. The girls all used to tease Dad mercilessly, and make him blush.

It was when he returned from Rhodes that he met and married my mother and we moved to Farnham. I don't know the exact details because my mother had a distant relationship with the truth – some of what she told me about those times may have been true but, equally, it could all have been a figment of her imagination.

He had always wanted to work in the theatre and ended up doing precisely that in Farnham. He got a job as stage manager and worked with the one and only Jessie Matthews. He toured with her in Pygmalion, and I still have a photograph of the two of them standing outside the theatre in Bath.

Mother was always a fantasist, who seldom told the truth about anything. Everything had to be heightened, exaggerated or changed completely. She was also a crashing snob who came from Birmingham and would ignore and even deny her family because they spoke with Brummie accents. Mum hated that accent and while it may not be everybody's cup of tea, it was part of who she was.

Her own mother, Agnes Baker, had gone to the Birmingham School of Art to do media work and her sister married George Maxwell, who was a member of the Eric Gill community in Ditchling in Sussex. Gill was a sculptor who set up a group for like-minded people, and George was a wood carver who made pews and images of saints and that kind of thing. My mother remembers people such as HG Wells coming along to visit the group. They were extraordinary people who all built their own houses. They lived a totally independent lifestyle, growing their own vegetables and suchlike, and keeping pigs and sheep.

The men would make pews and looms and the women would spin the wool and make their own clothes. In truth, it was the women who did most of the real work, while the men sat around at night discussing philosophy and the meaning of life. Gill, who was associated with the Arts and Craft movement, was a controversial figure whose religious views were at odds with his sexual behaviour and erotic art. He was a peculiar man who always wore a monk's habit, and he had lots of children. Unlike him, all his daughters always wore the latest fashion. Very strange, but it must also have been an exciting environment in which to grow up, surrounded by all these wonderfully artistic people.

When the Second World War broke out, my mother spent a lot of time with the Gill community because it was obviously safer for her to be with them than it was to be living in Birmingham. She had a cousin, Stephen, who joined the Gordon Highlanders and was killed in the war. Years later, I was in Aberdeen and I went to the Gordon Highlanders Museum to see if they could find out exactly what had become of him. It turned out that he was one of the thousands who died in the Battle of Monte Cassino and I was able to take Mum to his grave so that she could say goodbye properly. It was a deeply moving experience, and one that I will never forget.

Before the battle in Italy, the Gordon Highlanders also fought on the front line all across North Africa and suffered huge losses.

I made my first appearance on stage at Farnham Rep, as the infant Queen Elizabeth in *The Merry Wives of Windsor*. I was 18 months old. And when I was two years old, along came my sister, Maria. Like me, she was born in a nursing home in the village of Wrecclesham. I also have an elder half-sister by my mother's first marriage. Her name is Gail, and Mum walked out on her when she was just three years old. She literally left the house one day and never went back, leaving this poor little girl alone with her father.

I remember that our first house was a tiny cottage that we called 'The Kennel' because it was so small. It cost £600 but my parents could barely afford it because Dad earned only £8 a week in those days. Despite that, we had a pony in the back garden – my father always rode, and I ended up picking up his love of all things equine. We had a bathroom, but it had been tacked on to the end of the house and it was always freezing, especially so in the winter, when there would be frost on the inside of the windows and the water would turn to ice. One of my special treats was to have a hot bath in front of the fire. My sister and I both loved it.

My mother had an evil side, and I saw plenty of it during my childhood. She would whack us with anything that came to hand, including saucepans.

I suffered more than my fair share of emotional abuse at her hands, as did my sister. When I was growing up, I never felt that I was particularly good looking or especially talented because she was one of those people who could never offer praise. Nothing that I did was ever good enough for her.

She now has dementia and has turned into a sweet old lady, who thinks that I am quite wonderful. It was quite bizarre. I think: "It has taken all this time for you to treat me properly, to give me love and respect." And yet it wasn't really her; it was her condition that had turned her into the mother I had always dreamt of having.

During my formative years, all it would have taken was an arm round my shoulder, or to hear the words: "I love you," or "I am so proud of you." Was it really so very difficult for her to say? Well, clearly it was. Mother had been an only child, whose father died when she was about 15, and it had a profound effect upon her.

Thankfully, my Dad was everything that my mother wasn't. He was kind, caring and loving, and I consider myself very lucky to have had him.

Then there was Aunt Alice. She wasn't really an aunt, but a neighbour who happened to have two daughters who were older than me, and I always ended up wearing their hand-me-downs. All mothers will remember that one of the things they had to do was sew name tags into clothes, but my mother never did bother to replace the ones that came with Alice's children's clothes. She used to tell the teachers: "It's fine. She knows who she is."

My mother wasn't all bad. One thing I have to give her credit for is teaching me to read, something I was able to do by the time I was ready to start nursery school. It gave me a head start over most of the other children in my class. I was the youngest member of Farnham library, aged three years, and just used to devour books. I could not get through them quickly enough.

Mum and Dad had a bungalow built at Rushmoor, near Frensham Common – they employed the slowest builders in the world because it took two years to complete, but it was worth waiting for because it was in the middle of a wood, in the most beautiful setting that you could possibly imagine. I adored it, apart from one thing – mother had a wooden floor put down, but then she wouldn't let any of us walk on it. She spent the whole time screaming at us: "Get out! Get out! You will mark the floor." We always had to stand in the porch and take off our shoes and socks before coming into the house. In the end, I used to get in and out through my bedroom window because I worked out that it was the best way to ensure I could get a quiet life.

There was no heating in the property, and during the winter ice would form on the inside of the windows. Of course, it was the same for everybody back in the 1950s and 1960s. We take central heating for granted now but we used to freeze during the winters, I can tell you.

The heating used to come from a little electric fire in my bedroom, and I can still remember getting dressed under the bed clothes. On the up side, however, we had a fair bit of land, so we always had chickens, rabbits, dogs and ponies, and I loved that. Animals have always played a special part in my life, and not just because of my work.

When I was about six, Dad went for an interview with the BBC at Alexandra Palace and they offered him a job as a floor manager. Television was in its infancy back then, and those were very exciting times for everybody who was involved with it. There was a sense that they were all pioneers, in at the start of something extra special.

I remember Dad working on a production of *Jesus of Nazareth* starring a wonderful actor called Tom Fleming – it was a huge challenge, all the more so because everything was filmed live. They needed some children for the scene 'Suffer little children. Come unto me...' and the request went out: "Has anybody got any kids?"

"I've got a couple," said Dad.

"Okay, bring them in then."

My sister screamed the place down and had to be taken home, but I took to it like a duck to water. All that I had to do was walk up to Jesus and sit on his knee. I had to do it on a Thursday, and was back in again on the Sunday, and I loved it. I can recall thinking: "This is for me. This is what I want to do. I want to become an actress like Hayley Mills."

That was my moment. From that second I just knew, and I even told my parents, who reminded me that I had to go to school and get an education. It all seemed a bit inconvenient if I am honest. School? I was fairly certain that Hayley Mills did not go to school.

I was told that it was very difficult to get into acting and that maybe I should think about something else, but was I resolute in my determination. "Hayley Mills does it, so why can't I?" I am certain that there were thousands of other little girls all over Britain saying more or less precisely the same thing to their parents.

When I was nine years old I went to the girls' school in Farnham, and around the same time I got a pony called Mousy – she was a brilliant animal, whom I loved dearly. And so began my love affair with ponies and horses. I just adored going out riding, feeling the fresh air in my face. And I didn't care what the weather was like – it could be pouring down with rain, but it made no difference to me, just as long as I was able to ride.

I would ride at every available opportunity, especially during the school holidays. I even went hunting with her at weekends. It was not just me who loved it – Mousy did too. During the summer we used to compete in gymkhanas, taking part in show jumping competitions. She wasn't too keen on that, and used to let me know from time to time, but she put up with it. There was a brief period where I thought that I might want to become a top showjumper, but that didn't last long. Acting was always going to win out at the end of the day.

Everybody has teachers that make an impression, good or bad, and the one I remember was an English teacher called Miss Eggar. She inspired me to love English and to devour books. It wasn't difficult for her because, as I have already said, my parents had also encouraged me to read books from a very early age. I was reading Dickens and Kipling when I was ten years old. I had won a prize at school, a copy of *Our Mutual Friend*, by Charles Dickens and that led me to read everything else he had ever written.

But Miss Eggar was a special teacher who obviously saw something in me because she used to make sure that I appeared in all the school plays, and I was completely hooked. I fell in love with performing in front of an audience. Even as a child, it was what brought me to life and flicked on the switch inside me.

Mother wasn't keen on going to the theatre, but it was Dad's great passion and he took me to see the Olivier Season at Chichester. I may only have been 15 but I knew that this man up on stage was a special talent. Looking back on it, I find it hard to believe – apart from Olivier, I also saw Maggie Smith and Derek Jacobi, all giants of British theatre. Can you imagine sitting in a theatre watching Olivier and Maggie Smith in *Othello*? Just thinking about it now sends a shiver down my spine.

On another occasion I was watching Joan Plowright in *Saint Joan* and she had given such an astonishingly powerful performance that I was in tears, sobbing away. Dad gave me his handkerchief and then I realised that the old lady sitting on the other side of me was also crying, so after I had dried my eyes I gave her the hankie. At the end of the show, she said to me: "That was just as he wanted it to be." Then I realised that I had spent the performance sitting next to Cybil Thorndike. And she would have known, because Shaw wrote the part especially for her.

Dad did well at the BBC and moved up the ranks to become a producer-director. It was a big deal for him, and it was clear that he had found his niche, something that he loved and was really good at.

He worked in children's and adult drama, and was like a child in a sweet shop because he got to write the scripts, as well as producing and directing. It was a dream job really. He did a wonderful series about Rudyard Kipling called *Tales From The Hills*, *Sherlock Holmes* and even *Mr Pastry*, a wonderful slapstick creation for children starring Richard Hearne – you can still watch classic clips of the show on YouTube, and it remains as funny today as it was back then.

Hearne's comic timing was superb. I appeared in an episode of *Mr Pastry*. It involved me having to do a spectacular fall from my pony, and I had been practising it for ages, perfecting it. So I did it for the programme and everybody told me how brilliant I was, so then I thought that it might be fun to become a stuntwoman. The absolute truth is that the reason I wanted to become a stuntwoman was because I thought it would give me a chance to perform in front of the cameras while riding or falling off a horse – both my passions rolled into one.

Most of the BBC filming took place in the studios, but it seemed that whenever they needed an outside location that they ended up near our house, and there were countless scenes involving little girls skipping past the cameras – well, one little girl in particular.

When I was about 13 my grandfather died, so my grandmother moved to Farnham and I used to spend every Wednesday with her. At that time, Dad had one of the first Mini Coopers, which went like the clappers, and he used to have to get to and from London on the A3, but he could do it in 40 minutes because there were no speed limits and, best of all, there were hardly any other cars on the road. I dread to think how long that same journey would take now.

In 1965, Dad announced that he had been offered a job in Australia and we were all going to be emigrating. I wasn't quite sure precisely where Australia was, but I knew that it was a long, long way from England.

Just before we left, something extraordinary happened. Gail, the daughter from Mum's first marriage, tracked us down. I remember Mum saying to me: "Liza, this girl is your sister." Before I had a chance to get used to the idea, or even to get to know her, we were off, heading for a new life Down Under. I would get back in touch with her later and I now see her quite often. There is only five years between us and we have quite a lot in common. I could never understand why my mother treated Gail the way she did. It seemed extraordinarily cruel to me that anybody could do that to their own daughter.

They never really had a proper reconciliation until quite recently when Gail went to visit her at the home where she is now being looked after, and Mum apologised to her. "I am so sorry for everything I did to you," she said, and they both cried and cried and cried. It was an extraordinarily cathartic moment, and one of healing for Gail.

CHAPTER 2
THE LAND DOWN UNDER

"Yevgeny Yevtushenko, the Russian poet, drank champagne from my shoe. The romanticism of it all was lost on me. All I could say was: 'He's ruining my shoe. How disgusting is that?'"

My parents fostered two children, Beth and Margy, who had come from a Catholic home, but not long afterwards came Dad 's job offer – and what an offer it was too. They wanted him to become head of drama for the Australian Broadcasting Commission. It was 1965 and it was the opportunity of a lifetime because it gave him the chance to get in at the beginning of a fledgling television station.

And then, of course, there was the attraction of living in Australia, with all that wonderful weather. So yes we had to emigrate, but at least we were going to be living in a country where everybody else spoke English – after a fashion! The downside to all of this was that the foster children's mother would not allow my parents to take the kids Down Under, so they had to go back to the home.

Life didn't turn out too badly for them in the end, and I ended up catching up with Margy many years later and staying with her – in Australia of all places. By an amazing coincidence, Beth also lives in

Australia now.

But when we headed off to Australia we all felt terrible because we had no way of knowing what would become of the girls. Of course, we were not the only Poms on the ship – this was the time of the £10 package, where families left their lives behind in Britain and set sail in search of a new and better life Down Under. And for many people, Australia did indeed turn out to be the land of milk and honey. Then, like now, there were skill shortages so they were crying out for all sorts of craftsmen.

Dad went out there with his own unique set of skills, and we were all terribly excited about what we would find when we got there.

Dame Joan Sutherland, the opera singer, was performing in Sydney, and with her she had an amazing Italian tenor she had discovered. He went on to do rather well for himself. You may have heard of him – his name was Luciano Pavarotti and he had a spellbinding voice.

It was one of the biggest things to hit Sydney in years, and we were all invited to a party hosted by actor John McCallum and his wife Googie Withers – I should explain that McCallum was an Australian actor who met, fell in love with and married Googie, the renowned English actress, and they settled down together in Australia, where they were an active part of that amazing city's social scene. Theirs was one of the great show-business romances – they were married in 1948 and remained together until 2010, when John died.

So, who should be there at the party but Dame Joan and Pavarotti. There haven't been many times in my life when I have been starstruck, but that was most certainly one of them.

Luciano would later cook spaghetti for me in the flat where he was staying. I was very innocent in those days and it never once entered my head that he might have had ulterior motives, but he most certainly did.

Although he was a very attractive man in those days, possessed of enormous charisma, there was no way that anything was going to happen between us. Quite apart from anything else, I was a teenage girl, and he was a man, fully 15 years older than me, and maybe even more than that. Nevertheless, I was extremely flattered that this supremely talented individual should want to have his wicked way with me.

It didn't take my father long to make his mark, and he was soon producing some wonderful dramas, including one called *Love and War*, a full-scale production, the likes of which had never been tackled before in Australia. He would also go on to get involved in helping to set up the Australian film industry.

I was 15 when I got a job in a shop and moved into a flat with a girlfriend, and I spent as much time as I could going to the opera. I befriended one of the dancers, a woman called Renee, who was the wife of the great Canadian bass singer Joe Rouleau, and she made sure that I could get into the cast box at the Royal Opera House in Sydney whenever I wanted. As far as I was concerned, it was the hottest ticket in town. I saw all the great operas close-up and it was absolutely spellbinding for me. I felt as if I had died and gone to heaven.

Joan Sutherland was a remarkable performer. When she started to sing it did weird things to your brain – she was a big woman and she was no beauty either, but in front of your very eyes she would turn into this beautiful young girl dying of consumption, or whatever else the role called for her to be. She was utterly convincing. It was a rare gift and, in my opinion, she was the greatest opera singer the world has ever produced.

I got to meet her fairly frequently because the circles in which she moved in Sydney were pretty small, and always seemed to include John and Googie and my father. Googie would never go out in the Australian sun without a parasol. Whenever she went outside she always headed straight for the shade.

Dame Joan said to me once: "With the ribcage you have, my dear, you should have singing lessons." Although I was entranced by opera, it never entered my head that it might be a good idea to have lessons – I have had them since, of course, but I could have given myself such a head start back then if only I'd had the foresight. Now I think to myself: "Liza, what an idiot you were not to have done it."

I met Yevgeny Yevtushenko, the Russian poet, who drank champagne from my shoe. The romanticism of it all was lost on me. All I could say was: "He's drinking champagne from my shoe and he is ruining my shoe. How disgusting is that?" This was one of the great poets and all I could think of was that I might have to go out and buy a new pair of shoes. I was hopeless.

This was a pretty lofty world for a 16 year old English girl to become a part of, but anybody who was anybody went to John and Googie's parties. In the end, I suppose that I began to take it all for granted. It was just the way it was.

Through it all I was still determined to become an actress, and I landed a small part in a film called *They're a Weird Mob*, starring Walter Chiari and Chips Rafferty about an Italian immigrant (Chiari) who arrives in Australia with the promise of a job as a journalist on his cousin's newspaper. Chiari pursued me for some time and would endlessly phone me at home to ask me out – it took a long time before he finally got the hint that I just wasn't interested. He was about 35 years old and he just seemed ancient to me.

Then I got work as an assistant stage manager at The Old Tote

Theatre, which no longer exists, and I began to pick up small parts on a fairly regular basis. The job title was just a glorified alternative for being a dogsbody, but it didn't matter to me because I loved it. I was mixing with actors and theatre people. This was where I was meant to be and this was what I was born to do. I knew what to expect because during the school holidays back in Farnham, I had worked for the local theatre when I was 14. I was under no illusions.

My first part was as a daughter in *Inadmissible Evidence* – it wasn't the most taxing or demanding of roles because it didn't actually call upon me to say anything. Then, in 1966 when I was 16, I played Juliet in *Romeo and Juliet* for ABC television. It was a production that won several awards, and I was on my way. I then played Sophocles' Antigone – there was a long speech at the end, and we were filming it at night in a quarry in the pouring rain, and my lasting memory is of crawling along in front of a camera, saying my lines while I was soaked to the skin.

And then there was a TV series called *Something Else* – and it was. It was set in a hotel, to which pop stars came to stay. I say pop stars, but none of them would have been heard of outside Australia. So I was doing a lot of work and considered myself to be a serious actress.

Although Dad was an important figure in Australian television, he had no part in helping me to get work, which was the way both of us wanted it to be. I had to know that if I was given a role, then it was because I had earned it on my own merits, not because I was my father's daughter. In fact, more often than not I would go for parts and not even tell him I was going for an audition. I felt it was better to keep quiet until I knew that I had been offered something.

In many ways I may have been naïve but I was full of self-confidence when I was 16-17 years old, as you tend to be because at that point you haven't suffered the rejections or the 'Don't call us, we'll call you...' You feel invincible.

This was the time of the Vietnam War and we lived in King's Cross, which was the heart of the red light district – when the soldiers got rest and recuperation (R&R), this was where they headed, so there always seemed to be hundreds of them milling about. I remember my father complaining once that the door in the house below had been banging all night long – it wasn't the door. It turned out that we were living above a whorehouse and what Dad could hear was the garden gate.

Mother twigged on pretty quickly and announced: "We can't possibly stay here." The other thing, of course, was that I was always being propositioned by soldiers and sailors because they figured that if I lived in this area then I was fair game.

We moved to an area called Avalon, which wasn't a lot better if I am honest, but the local beach was just gorgeous. It was soon afterwards that I moved into my own flat in Sydney, but I would go back to see my parents most weekends, and spend almost the entire time on the beach and in the sea. It was beautiful.

Mother found herself a job, working as a receptionist for a sports medicine specialist – even back in those days, the Australians were way ahead of the game when it came to looking after their athletes. This specialist looked after the Australian Olympic team and was very highly regarded.

Because of the presence of all these service personnel I became interested in the Vietnam War and started to read up on it. It wasn't long before I formed the opinion that it was a pretty pointless conflict, and I realised that millions of other people around the world felt much the same way. There were regular protests and demonstrations against the war and felt so strongly about it all that I joined them.

Mother joined an organisation called Catholic Women and Girls Against the War, and on one occasion I joined her on a protest march and we were water-cannoned, right in the heart of Sydney. When they opened fire on us with the water, the force was such that we were all be swept off our feet – when you had been water-cannoned once, you made sure it never happened to you again.

Taking part in protest marches was not seen as the thing to do, but I had friends, aged 18, who were getting their telegrams to tell them that they had been called up to serve in Vietnam. The thing is that nobody seemed to know what the war was all about, and from a very early stage, most analysts worked out that it was not a conflict that anybody could win.

I may have felt differently if people had been left to volunteer, but I just felt that conscription was wrong if it meant that young boys were immediately flown into a country where they could lose their lives fighting for a cause they neither understood nor cared anything about. The Americans had taken it upon themselves to go into Vietnam, so why should innocent Australian teenagers be asked to sacrifice their lives?

It had nothing to do with Australia, and it would not surprise me if, even now, the vast majority of people living around the world do not know that the Aussies were dragged into the conflict.

My sister's boyfriend received a telegram telling him to report for duty. It was a dreadful time, and I vividly recall the tearful farewells, and her saying that she would never see him again. But a couple of days later, he was back home. He had spent half his life on a surfboard, wearing nothing on his feet, and he had terrible calluses all over his feet (called board bumps Down Under), the result of which was that he failed his army medical. There was much rejoicing upon his return, as you can imagine.

CHAPTER 3
SKIPPY

*"It used to become unbearably hot when we were filming inside the house –
there was a sound man who used to have to stand at the top of a ladder with
his sound boom, and he frequently used to faint and fall off his ladder. It was
miraculous that he was never seriously injured."*

By 1967, I had managed to scrape enough money together to buy myself
a car, a VW Beetle. I had found myself an agent, who sent me for an
audition for a part in what was going to be a new series. The brainchild
of John McCallum, it was called *Skippy The Bush Kangaroo*, and it changed
my life forever.

Before we started filming, my beloved grandmother had died and I
had been given some of her belongings, including a fabulous pair of
earrings, but they were for pierced ears, and I hadn't had mine done at
that point, so my mother told me to come down to centre where she
worked, saying that the physiotherapist would pierce my ears.

It was an experience I will never forget. The physio had muscles on
top of muscles and he took a cork from a wine bottle of my father's and
placed it on one side of my ear and then took a needle and proceeded to
push it through my ear lobe until it sank into the cork. There was blood
everywhere and it hurt like hell. Naturally, I was shrieking and

screaming – waiting to come in and see him were a number of footballers who must have been wondering what form of torture was being inflicted upon me. They must have thought he was performing a do-it-yourself abortion. And it didn't help when I emerged with blood pouring from my ears. All this to save a few Australian dollars.

Of course, he did them 'on the wonk', as they say in Norfolk – one hole was higher than the other. And then my ears decided to swell up, and were still swollen during my first day of filming. It wasn't a particularly auspicious start to my television career.

I originally signed up to do six episodes but ended up staying in the series for two years, and it took over my life. They didn't do things in half-measures in Australia – the first series consisted of a mind-boggling 39 episodes.

This was a full-on commitment. I was working six days a week, from six in the morning until six in the evening, usually in the most incredibly hot conditions with the sun beating down all day long. I am not complaining, but it is a fact that it was hard work. The series was shot in northern Sydney at the Ku-ring-gai Chase National Park, and for me and the rest of the cast it was just a job.

I have to tell you that I had no sense or feeling that I was in at the start of something special. I don't think that any of us, cast or production team, felt that we had a big hit on our hands. It was a time when there seemed to be a proliferation of children's television programmes and movies featuring animals and creatures of various shapes and sizes that always seemed to be able to save the day – there was *Champion The Wonder Horse*, *Rin Tin Tin* (a dog), *Flipper* the dolphin and, of course, the daddy of them all, *Lassie*.

Why would a programme featuring a kangaroo that could only be understood by a young boy be a success? But that is one of the great mysteries, and also one of the attractions, of television – there are no sure-fire winners. If there were, life would be far simpler. Some shows have a special something, others are right for the time and then there are the ones that grab the imagination and nobody really knows why.

Lee Robinson, one of the producers, had a house built that formed the set – we either filmed there or outside. The plan was that Lee was going to live in the house afterwards – well, it was only going to be a short series of six episodes after all, so why wouldn't he be able to go and live in it? It used to become unbearably hot when we were filming inside the house – there was a sound man who used to have to stand at the top of a ladder with his sound boom, and he frequently used to faint because of the heat, and fall off his ladder. It was miraculous that he was never seriously injured.

They weren't big on health and safety back then. On one occasion there were bush fires raging all around us so the director said: "Okay everybody, we may as well film inside today." There was no question of us leaving the area, even though the sky was black because there was so much smoke. Bush fires are extremely dangerous, and can easily get out of hand, and there was an episode we filmed that featured one – nobody sought permission to start it and it very nearly did get out of control. The authorities would have a fit if such a thing happened today, but nobody ever seemed to think about the possible consequences.

TV in Australia back then was in black and white, but the series was filmed in colour in order to increase its marketability around the world and it worked, as it was shown in America and Canada between 1969 and 1972, and it was the most popular series in Japan. The Nine Network in Australia was to repeat it when colour arrived Down Under in 1975. It was also dubbed into Spanish and became a big hit in Mexico, where it was known as *Skippy el canguro*. Unbelievably, it was shown in Czechoslovakia in the 1970s and 1980s, and is still being shown in Iran today. Almost equally unbelievably, the authorities in Sweden banned the show because psychologists believed it would mislead children into thinking they could get animals to do whatever they wanted.

The lead characters were Matt Hammond (played by Ed Devereaux), the Head Ranger of Waratah National Park, Sonny Hammond (Garry Pankhurst), who was Matt's youngest son, Mark Hammond (Ken James), who was Matt's oldest son, and Jerry King (Tony Bonner), who played the helicopter pilot.

I played the part of Clarissa 'Clancy' Merrick, the teenage daughter of a ranger stationed at another section of the Waratah National Park. When her father is transferred to a park in northern New South Wales, Matt invites Clancy to stay with the Hammond family so that her music studies are not disrupted by the move north.

The stories revolved around events in the park, including its animals, dangers arising from natural hazards in the park's environment, and the actions of visitors to the park. The absence of a 'Mrs Hammond' (Sonny and Mark's mother) was explained as being due to her death when Sonny was a young child.

It all seemed pretty straightforward – girl falls down well, Skippy comes across girl, bounds back across the outback and finds Sonny, who is the only one who can understand him, tells Sonny about girl trapped down the well, Sonny gets his Dad, they all head back to the well, girl is pulled out and they all live happily ever after. It wasn't rocket science, but the children of Australia loved it and it was a smash hit from day one.

Skippy communicated with Sonny by making clicking sounds – it would be wonderfully romantic to be able to say that they were genuine kangaroo noises but they were actually vocal sound effects, made the sound engineer. Skippy's apparent manual dexterity was not what it seemed either. We had to use real kangaroo arms stuck on the end of sticks in the hands of human operators. In the end you could buy them in the shops and they became quite popular. They did make very good back scratchers though.

Kangaroos are not especially lovable creatures and cannot be tamed so we always had to have about 20 of them on set. If we hadn't done that they would simply have bounded off into the outback, never to be seen again.

The daily routine did not change much. I would get up at 5am, wash my hair and then head into make-up, where I would be given my scenes for the day.

Life back in the flat in the Paddington area was fairly colourful. We had a gay man living in the property – his name was Gaydon and he used to spend his life wandering around in prison clothes. There was a lesbian living downstairs and a hippy who slept in a room next to the bathroom – on one occasion he called me down and said: "Can you come and have a look at this please?" He had a huge mark on his side and it turned out to be the worst case of ringworm that I had ever seen. It was like a dinner plate on the side of his body and I told him that he had to go and see a doctor immediately.

One time all the lights went out, but we had a group of anarchists living next door and they were brilliant – before we knew what had happened, they had the power working again. It turned out that the fuses had blown but Gaydon, the lesbian and the hippy hadn't the foggiest idea what to do, and neither did I.

I painted my room black and put up pink and orange curtains – can you imagine what it looked like? I thought it was gorgeous. Then again, it was the 1960s.

I decided that the time had probably come to find somewhere else to live and moved into a house in the Surrey Hills area of Sydney which I shared with a lovely girl called Barbara Joss, whose father was a famous newspaper cartoonist in England. There was a peach tree in the garden, and each morning I used to pick a peach and eat it on my way to work.

There were still Aborigines living in the area and, once again, prostitutes. I don't know why, but I always seemed to end up living in red light districts. One of the prostitutes had an Alsatian and I used to look after it at night because she was otherwise engaged. My lasting memory of the Aborigines was that they were feckless individuals who did nothing, but they were lovely people. And then the authorities cleared them out of Sydney, which made my blood boil. It was no different to the apartheid that was rife in South Africa at the time and in many ways it was worse – this was their land after all.

I had seen apartheid in action. When we moved to Australia we went by ship, and it stopped off in South Africa on the way. It was a real eye-opener for a young girl from Surrey. I could not believe how badly the black population were treated – it was as if they were animals. They couldn't go into certain shops, they could not walk on the same pavements as the whites, they couldn't get on the same buses, and they couldn't use the same public toilets. I was appalled by what I saw during the short stop-over.

We spent some time on a beautiful beach and, of course, there was not a black person to be seen. I asked where they went if they wanted to come to the beach and was pointed towards an area that was miles away from where we were – somewhere that could only be reached by car and none of these people could afford to buy a car, so they never got to enjoy the simple pleasure of being able to spend a day of a beach.

I remember being stopped as I was about to walk into a public toilet and being told I could not use it.

"Why not?" I asked.

"Because it's a black-only toilet. You need to use that one over there."

"This isn't right," I thought to myself. And I thought precisely the same thing again when the Australians were kicking the Aborigines out of Sydney and sending them off into the Northern Territories. "You can't do this." But they did. To witness at first hand that sort of persecution left its mark on me, and has remained with me for the rest of my life. I cannot bear the thought of social injustice.

It was like the way that the Americans treated their native people – they stuck them on reservations with other tribes with whom they had nothing in common, and gave them land that was nothing like where they had come from. And so it was with the Aborigines. They were treated like dirt. The attitude was: "Well look at their ancestors – they had the land for thousands of years and they did nothing with it." That was because they were in tune with their surroundings – they lived off the land, killing animals only for food, not for sport.

It is only now that the Aborigines are being treated as equals, and being shown the respect they deserve. But they suffered terribly. One of the major problems was their intolerance to alcohol – again, just like the indigenous Americans; they have never been able to digest it properly so you ended up with a situation where they were perceived as drunken layabouts. I used to think it was an old wives' tale but there are lots of people around the world for whom alcohol almost acts as a type of poison, such as the Polynesians.

I have strayed from the point but I believe it is important to give you a feel for what Australia was like at the time. Don't get me wrong, there were lots of Australians who felt the same as me about the way the Aborigines were being treated.

One episode of *Skippy* featured me falling off my horse, and I was to be rescued by a group of Aborigines, who had been flown in from the Northern Territories. They were a lovely group of people (a 20-strong dance troupe), but they were made to sleep on camp beds in an old aircraft hangar. The most striking thing about this was that they were so used to being treated in this way that they accepted it without question, even though everybody else had proper beds.

They had a minder with them, a dreadful individual wearing sweat-stained clothes, and we had to ask for his permission to take them on a night out with the cast and crew. They got all dressed up and looked fantastic and we went into town and went to a club and I asked: "Is it all right if we bring the boys in?"

"Yes, of course it is, but he can't come in." And so it was that the minder was left outside.

So where was I? Oh yes, *Skippy*. The six episodes ended up becoming 92. I suppose that myself and the rest of the cast became pretty famous in Australia but we hardly ever got the chance to find out what impact it was to have on our lives because we spent so much time working so, at the most, we could go out once a week and even then we had to be back home at a sensible time because we all had to be up with the lark for work.

I would sometimes go to a club with Tony Bonner and all the girls would swoon over him. But they weren't like that because he was a famous actor – they were all over him because he was a really good looking young man. Some nights we would also all head to the beach.

I've got to say, however, that although it was a successful show, we weren't followed by hordes of autograph hunters or anything like that. Back then, nobody got terribly excited about television stars, certainly not in Australia. It was quite a laid-back life out there and people didn't make a fuss.

We had some famous guest stars, including Mark McManus, the Scottish actor who would go on to make a name for himself as the Glaswegian police detective Jim Taggart. Between scenes, the kangaroos used to be kept in sacks – it may sound cruel but they were perfectly happy because it reminded them of their mother's pouch. And when it got really hot, the crew would sprinkle the sacks with cold water to keep the animals cool. Mark came on set, pointed to the bag and asked: "What is that?"

"Oh don't worry Mark; it's only one of the kangaroos."

"What? Well if that is how you treat the star of the show, what do you do to the guest artists?"

Then there was a larger than life gay actor called Frank Thring, whose claim to fame was that he had been in *Ben Hur* as Pontius Pilate and in one scene he was filmed still wearing his wristwatch. He said of Charlton Heston, the star of *Ben Hur*: "Ah yes, Chuck. He had delusions of adequacy."

The food we were served on set was dreadful, so Frank used to get his butler to bring him a hamper every day. It was filled with the most amazing delicacies, including champagne, which he would proceed to drink before going back to work. I had never seen anything like it before – here, in front of my eyes, was a genuine Hollywood star, and I was working with him. Life surely didn't get much better than this.

An interesting footnote about Frank is that his father was credited with inventing the clapperboard.

Anybody who was anybody in the acting profession in Australia appeared on *Skippy* at some stage or other.

I had a love-hate relationship with the kangaroos. Some of them were lovely animals, including one called Stumpy, who was so named because he had a couple of fingers missing, but most of them were not. As I have already said, it was difficult to tame a kangaroo and it was impossible to get one to do what you wanted it to, so you can imagine how many takes we had to do.

While putting them in sacks may not have been cruel, some things did go on that would never be allowed to happen today. In an attempt to keep the kangaroos from hopping off, the crew would get hold of a big leather strap and tie it to the animal's tail. So we would be doing a scene and there would be a prop man lying on the floor out of camera shot, holding the animal's tail with all his might to stop it from bouncing off. We also did a lot of filming in the house with the kangaroos – they pooed and had a wee everywhere. It was almost as if they were all incontinent. And can you imagine the smell? When that was combined with the heat, it made most of us feel like we were about to throw up.

The most striking thing was that they always wanted to bound away, which was only natural really. I could never understand why the producers did not build a fence to keep them in – there was nothing to stop them escaping and you can call me old-fashioned if you like, but if you are a wild animal and you see a chance to bounce off into what is your natural habitat, then you are going to take it.

It was great training for a young actress. Every time we did a scene, there was enormous pressure on all the actors to get it right in one go and then, if the kangaroo did something dreadful, we would have to do it all over again. When the animal got right or, rather, did what was wanted, that would always be the scene that was used, so woe betide the actor who messed up. One of my lasting memories of the series would be watching the entire crew running after a kangaroo that had decided it had had enough and was going to make a bolt for freedom. It was hilarious, and it led to some very frayed tempers.

The camera would usually be left running, so I would go over and turn it off. There was a bottle of whisky given to the crew members who brought back the most kangaroos every week.

One of the other most striking things about *Skippy* was that I was the only girl in the cast. And there were only three on the crew – one in wardrobe, one in continuity and the other in make-up. So that was fairly intimidating, especially in the early days of shooting. In the end, I just became one of the boys. We were cut off from the outside world, living in a sort of fantasy land.

Being on a film set is an amazing experience anyway, but for a teenager, as I was at the time it was also a great way to learn. I loved the banter and somebody always seemed to be cracking jokes, so there were lots of laughs to go along with all the hard work. I couldn't believe my luck. I had always wanted to be actress and here I was appearing in one of the best shows on Australian television.

When all was said and done, Skippy was a children's programme so there wasn't a great deal of critical acclaim, not even from my parents. I had stated that I wanted to become a classical actress and this was anything but that. If you watch it now, the thing that will strike you is how sweet and innocent it all was.

Garry was only 11 years old and he was a divine child, but he had to have education, so there was a tutor on the set. And there were also restrictions applied to how much filming he could do each day.

There was one scene in which I was holding a wombat, and had a baby koala bear on one shoulder and a possum on the other, and Garry had a snake wrapped round him, holding the head in one hand and the tail in the other. We asked if it was poisonous and were told that it wasn't. The possum didn't know that, however, and it was terrified so it had a wee all over my shoulder. There was no change of clothing and nowhere to dry my top, so I ended up drying it under a stage light, but that didn't get rid of the smell. When it came to lunchtime, nobody would sit next to me.

We finally got ready to do the scene for real, and what they hadn't told us was that although the snake wasn't poisonous, it was a constrictor and it started to wrap itself around Garry's neck and squeeze. He was turning blue in front of me, but we had all been trained to carry on acting until the director said, "Cut," so that is what we did. Eventually, it was obvious to everybody what was happening, and the crew dived in and removed the snake from Garry's neck.

As if that wasn't bad enough, I then discovered that I had caught lice from the animals. John McCallum was furious and when we came in the next day it looked as if it had been snowing – in fact, all the animals had been covered in louse powder.

There was another occasion my character had to be rescued after getting her foot caught in a rock as the tide was starting to come in. Eventually the water went over her head and she had to breathe through a tube until good old Skippy rescued her. The thing is that they needed somebody to stand in the water, let it go over her head and then breathe through a tube, and there were no stunt doubles, so I had to do it myself. We knew that the water was shark-infested and I asked what was going to be done about the sharks.

"Don't worry Liza; somebody will keep an eye out for them."

I was not terribly reassured. If somebody spotted a shark, how were they going to ensure that it did not have me for lunch? Nobody was able to give me an answer to that one. In the end, I spent hours and hours in the water and finished up in hospital for a week suffering from exposure.

Apart from the snakes we had on set, we were working in an environment where deadly poisonous snakes and spiders made their homes, so we always had to be on our guard. We knew which ones to look out for and avoid, and it reached the point where we would be filming and would be walking along delivering our lines and would see one of these snakes curled up on the ground – in the early days it might have more natural for me to have screamed; instead we learned that if we caused a vibration on the ground with our feet, the snakes would slither off into the undergrowth. They were more scared of us than we were of them, although I would never have wanted to put it to the test, and one of the legacies of my days on *Skippy* is that I still walk with my eyes to the ground all the time.

On one occasion I walked into the ladies toilet and discovered that it was where a brown snake had given birth to its babies, so I flew out shouting: "There's a snake in the loo, and it's had loads of babies."

The response? "Well don't go in there then, Liza."

So we ended up having to pee in the bushes. And while we were doing so, the cameramen would film us and when the rushes were shown each day, guess what would always be included? All the men would screech with laughter.

There was also an emu, and I am convinced that our emu was the one that Rod Hull based his act upon. They used to have to bring it on set in a wheelbarrow, with somebody sitting astride it to prevent it from running away. This was a seriously bad-tempered bird, but then somebody discovered that it had a taste for whisky and after a couple of mouthfuls, it became transformed. It actually calmed down and tolerated people. The downside to this was that it would have a hangover in the morning and would be worse than ever for the first couple of hours every day. It was a vile creature.

We had a wombat that was kept in a cage and if anybody was stupid enough to put a hand into the cage, it would try and take off their fingers. On the other hand, there were koala bears everywhere, and they were just divine. Now, of course, their numbers have been greatly reduced because mankind has destroyed so much of their habitat, as well as the virus that has wiped out so much of the population, but it was very different 40-odd years ago.

I remember a baby koala coming into the house and falling asleep on the ironing board as I did the ironing. They just used to sit there and eat leaves, and if they weren't eating, they were sleeping, but they were adorable, and were completely docile. I have seen koalas remain in the exact same spot for an entire day. Every time I saw one I just wanted to give it a hug. They have that effect on most people.

Every so often, John McCallum and Googie would visit the set, arriving like royalty in their Rolls Royce. Funnily enough, when they were about, lunch was always good. As a matter of routine, they would serve us fish and chips in temperatures that regularly soared above 110F, and there would be flies everywhere. It was disgusting.

The TV series was so successful that the decision was taken to make a film, *Skippy and the Intruders*, and it was enormous fun. We all went to Victoria to shoot it and ended up staying in a wonderfully creepy old house.

The storyline revolved around head ranger Matt Hammond being approached by two divers for permission to search for abalone (sea snails) off the coast of the Waratah National Park, flight ranger Jerry king was suspicious. He was certain there were no abalone in Waratah, and, when he saw the divers' large cruiser, he was convinced they were not fisherman. He was right, it turned out that they had been hired to find a wreck and illegally salvage the cargo...naturally, Skippy saved the day.

Once again, Clancy had to be rescued from the water, but this time there was to be no exposure. My character seemed to spend most of her life being rescued, and it would always be the same line: "Go and get help Skippy," and this animal, which always seemed to be in the right place at the right time, would somehow always manage to find its way home to Garry and tell him that Clancy was in trouble. "What's that Skip? Clancy's in trouble again?" And with that the helicopter would be mobilised and Clancy would duly be rescued.

But this was different because it was a proper film – it ran for two hours and twenty minutes.

I did actually end up going fishing for abalone, but that wasn't a straightforward experience either. I had been told that we would be going in a proper fishing boat, but it turned out to be a speedboat that had been stripped of everything, apart from a crate that served as a seat and an enormous outboard engine, meaning that it went like a bat out of hell.

When he reached what he thought was a good point, my companion, who was a professional diver, stopped the boat and dived into the water, and my fishing trip consisted of me sitting on my crate watching him dive into the ocean and repeatedly come back up to the surface with these sea snails. It wasn't quite what I had expected or imagined. I have never been so bored in all my life.

They were regarded as a delicacy and I have to admit that I did try some and they were absolutely delicious. The Japanese pay big money for them.

Ed Devereaux, who played the ranger, had been a big star in musicals in London's West End, and he used to get drunk at parties and would always end up singing, and nobody could stop him until he had gone through the entire repertoire, singing all the songs from all the shows he had appeared in.

Because we were working so hard, the time just flew by and before I knew where I was, I had completed two years in *Skippy*, and the decision was taken that, after 92 half-hour episodes, it had run its course. But they had decided to film a new series, set on a sailing ship and filmed off the Great Barrier Reef, and I was asked if I wanted to appear in it, but I told them that I didn't because I felt it was about time that I returned to England.

CHAPTER 4
VIEW FROM A TRAIN

"Moscow was a grim and austere place, and everybody looked thoroughly miserable. While I was there I saw people being bundled into cars off the street by the KGB."

During the little spare time that I'd had, I discovered Russian novelists. I read *War and Peace* by Tolstoy and everything by Dostoevsky and it all made a deep impression upon me, so much so that I had made up my mind that I wanted to visit Siberia. I needed a holiday and I had money in the bank, so I decided to return to England via the Trans-Siberian express. To me, it was the equivalent of the Orient Express.

It was expensive. Even back then, the trip cost me around £2,000, but it was something I desperately wanted to do, and I have always believed that you should follow your heart and that if you have an opportunity to make a dream come true then you should grab it with both hands, rather than living a life and then saying: "If only..." I figure that you only get one shot at this, so you go for it.

I was leaving from Sydney, and my ultimate destination was London. I left Sydney and my first flight took me to Japan, and from Japan I caught a boat to Russia, then on to a train that took me all across Russia, from Russia to Finland, from Finland to Denmark, Denmark to Holland, across to West Berlin in Germany and then back to London. It was an epic journey, and it turned out to be everything that I'd hoped it would.

It was 1969, I was 19 years old and I travelled first class all the way. The carriages were like something from a bygone age – your bed was pulled down at night, and then an attendant would come round the following day and stow it away again.

We all had self-contained compartments, with a corridor outside, and at the end of each carriage worked a lady stoker, who piled coal on to a furnace to heat the carriages – it was as warm as toast all day, but what a job that must have been. And why it was done by a woman I have absolutely no idea.

I shared my compartment with a delightful male German student called Rolf Stoeker who was an absolute gentleman, and during the day we would sit and chat and be served tea in our coach. I felt utterly spoilt, even though I had paid for the privilege. We would go to sleep in one part of Russia and the train would carry on travelling through the night and when we awoke the following morning the landscape would have changed completely.

There were lots of students on the train and I had a great time talking to them all. We discussed Russian literature, history and politics, among other things. There was a priest who was travelling around the world and a political journalist who was writing about the differences between communism, capitalism and an oppressive regime. They were fascinating travelling companions.

We then discovered that we could trade in our food vouchers for brandy and cigarettes, and that is precisely what we did, and a good time was had by all as we seemed to spend a good deal of our time singing and dancing on the train. The food on board was awful, but at every station where we stopped there were women wearing head scarves who were selling food – there was a type of doughnut with mince inside that was absolutely delicious.

The train pulled into Khabarousk, which was packed with soldiers who were on their way to take part in a border conflict with the Chinese. We were staying in a local hotel that night, so we all poured off the train – I was wearing a mini-skirt and ended up dancing with the soldiers when all of a sudden this huge woman appeared and roared: "Niet!" Whereupon she took me by the arm, marched me to my room and locked me in. She was worried that I was going to land myself in hot water and get into trouble, but I am certain it would all have been absolutely fine.

There were a couple of girls on board, one of whom was due to get married and was taking part in a grand adventure before settling down. Somebody else had been working in Hong Kong. I was so lucky to have shared this trip with a tremendous bunch of people.

They were all getting off at Lake Baikal, so I decided to join them. Lake Baikal is located in south-east Siberia and it is the world's oldest (25 million years) and deepest (1,700 metres) lake, containing roughly 20% of the world's surface fresh water. It is home to more than 1,700 species of plants and animals, most of which can be found nowhere else in the world. As a result, it is known as Russia's Galapagos. The lake is surrounded by fabulous forests that stretch all the way to Mongolia. It is now a Unesco world heritage site, but such things were unheard of back then.

I wasn't supposed to get off at Lake Baikal. Back in those days you were given a visa, upon which were listed the towns and cities where you were allowed to visit, so I decided to get off and just play dumb. In the Russia of the time, I guess that it was a pretty foolhardy thing to do, but I didn't care because I was having such fun with all these great people.

As it turned out, the pull of the American dollar made everything all right. It would not have been recommended, or sensible, to try and bribe border guards and security people in Moscow, but in the rest of the country they were all pretty laid back and their eyes used to light up when they saw dollars, and I'd had the foresight to make sure that I had some with me.

It was April and although there wasn't a cloud in the sky, there was thick snow everywhere and the lake was frozen, so I was able to dance on the surface and drink champagne. Wow! What a fabulous, unforgettable experience that was.

Unfortunately, it had to come to an end and eventually we all had to get back on the train, but the party continued. And then, as we started to get closer to Moscow, we became aware that the train staff's attitude was changing. They became apprehensive and as we would pull into stations they would make sure that any drink and suchlike had been cleared away. Men carrying guns would get on the train at these stations and make their way through the carriages, checking everybody's papers, and it was quite clear that the waiters were absolutely terrified.

When we got to Moscow I was immediately struck by just what an awful city it was. The people of Siberia had been outgoing and friendly, but that all changed when we arrived in the capital. It was a grim and austere place, and everybody looked thoroughly miserable. While I was there I saw people being bundled into cars off the street by the KGB.

You may wonder how I knew they were the KGB. When you went into any restaurant or shop you had to take your coat off because they were so hot, especially so after being outside in the cold. But there were always these shady characters who kept their coats on, and I soon worked out that these were the KGB. They stuck out like sore thumbs, a bit like Hitler's Gestapo.

These men were everywhere, thousands of them. Our hotel rooms were bugged as a matter of routine, although what they thought they were going to pick up from a 19-year-old actress on her way back to England is anybody's guess. As I had been growing up and was reading books I had believed that Communism was the way forward. I soon realised that it was a naive, idealist view and that the reality of Communism was that it created a society of the haves and the have-nots, and the haves seemed to spend their entire existence spying on the have-nots to ensure that nothing changed in the grand order of things. It was all rather depressing.

Basically, the Russian people were oppressed, so my views changed very quickly. I looked around and told myself that it was wrong, that people could not live like this. They had nothing and, of course, the only people who had cars were the KGB and the members of the politbureau. The population had to rely on a creaking transport system, bikes or their own two legs. And they lived in horrible concrete boxes that resembled prison blocks. Was it any wonder they never smiled?

Then I went to Leningrad (now St Petersburg once more) and although the regime was still as rigid, it was chalk and cheese when compared with Moscow. Leningrad was a beautiful city. Apart from the main square, Moscow was a grim, grey place with little or nothing to commend it.

I visited the Hermitage Museum, which houses some of Russia's greatest works of art and, to my utter astonishment, I found that I just about had the entire place to myself. Local people didn't go to museums, and tourists were few and far between. That was an eerie experience.

And whereas in Moscow the hotels were pretty basic, to say the least, in St Petersburg they were magnificent buildings with glorious four-poster beds. I was in my element. The food was the same wherever I went though – not good.

My time is Russia eventually came to an end, and I left with a heavy heart, although I was delighted that I had fulfilled one of my life-long ambitions, and it had been everything I had hoped it would be, other than the sense of anti-climax I had felt when I realised that Communism simply did not work in real life.

Next on my agenda was Finland and it came as quite a culture shock to me – suddenly I was back in western civilisation and there were cars and lights and people making a noise and laughing in public. And there were restaurants that served proper food. One of my abiding memories of Finland is of the extraordinary amount of food that used to be piled up on the breakfast table. Compared to Russia, there was such abundance.

Finland was a beautiful country with lots of spectacular scenery. Next up was Denmark, where I met up with a group of Armenians, and ended up going back to their flat. In this day and age you expect to meet people who have uprooted everything and emigrated, but this was 1969, and I had barely heard of Armenia, far less met anybody who came from there. But like just about everybody else I had the good fortune to meet on that trip, they were really friendly people who wanted to share their lives with me, a complete stranger.

And so it was that I came to eat Armenian food for the first time in my life. I believe that part of the reason so many people opened their arms to me was because I was travelling on my own. When you have a companion with you, you are far less likely to mix with other people. On top of that, I was something of an extrovert and enjoyed talking to new people and making friends with complete strangers – I suppose that it might be different today, but in 1969 everything felt safe and secure.

Quite apart from anything else, as a 19-year-old, I had no fear. I felt invincible and did not regard what I was doing as anything out of the ordinary. Yes, it was an adventure, but it held no fears for me.

I arrived home in England, and it quickly became apparent to me that nobody knew anything about the conflict between the Russians and the Chinese, and that very few people were aware of what was happening in Vietnam, and those who did, simply didn't care. That all began to change with the release of films such as *The Deer Hunter* and suddenly everybody was appalled at what was happening.

I arrived in London as the place was exploding with colour, fashion and music. People talk about the swinging sixties, but most of it happened at the end of the decade, and I was there to soak it all in.But I had to find somewhere to live. Before we had moved to Australia, I had badgered my parents endlessly about my desire to be a performer and they eventually gave in and allowed me to attend the Arts Educational Trust in London, which was a drama and dance school, as well as providing normal education.

The way it worked was that we do standard classroom lessons in the morning, and drama and dance in the afternoon. It was based in a beautiful building at 144 Piccadilly, which is now the Intercontinental Hotel. One thing that sticks in my mind was the magnificent marble staircase.

I was there with Nigel Havers, Susie Blake and Jane Seymour, to name but a few. There were lots of extremely talented individuals, people whom I just knew would go on to become big stars. I loved it with a passion, even though I used to have to travel backwards and forwards by bus and train from Farnham on a daily basis. It meant setting off at six in the morning, but I loved it so much that I didn't care.

My parents had wonderful friends called Brenda Ulrich and David Burke, who lived in Belsize Park in London, and I lived with them during the week. I first met them when I was 13 years old. She was an exceptionally gifted portrait artist and he was a staunch member of the Communist Party in London who drove a limousine for a living. He was a fascinating character who was incredibly well-read. He knew all about music, art, literature and politics, and it was David who really got my interest in books going.

He was a close friend of Dora Russell, who was Bertrand Russell's widow. I met her and she told me that she had always regretted throwing Bertrand out after finding him in bed with a parlour maid. "How stupid I was," she said. "Imagine losing such a wonderful man over a mere parlour maid. I would never do that again."

Dora's father had believed with a passion that girls were entitled to have just as good an education as boys, and his influence rubbed off on her. She was an ardent feminist who was way ahead of her time, and she believed in sexual freedom. When Bertrand first proposed marriage to her, she refused, although she was willing to live with him. She saw marriage as a restriction on women's liberty, and although Bertrand accepted her philosophical argument on the subject, he wanted a son and legitimate heir to the family title.

She eventually agreed to marry him and after giving birth to her first child, she became involved in the birth control movement. Dora Russell

44

was a truly amazing woman, and it was a privilege to have met her.

Brenda's great pleasure in life was to paint the walls of her house, which she preferred to painting portraits. She taught me how to decorate, and also how to hang wallpaper. One day I went out and when I returned I nearly walked past the house – when I had left in the morning, the front door was black, but now it was bright pink. She was a marvellous role model, and every house I have lived in since then, I have done the decorating myself, apart from the cottage we live in today.

Brenda introduced me to the joys of art. She would take me to various galleries and exhibitions and we would look at pictures and she would wax lyrical and tell me all about them. It was another part of my education. Brenda was fascinated with painting miniatures, which is a remarkable skill that requires untold patience and attention to detail, and when David unearthed an 18th century book which described in detail how a miniature was painted, she was totally in her element.

When I had first met them they had just come back from travelling across Afghanistan in a camper van, which was another great dream of mine – I should have gone as part of my great adventure in 1969, and now it is too dangerous to contemplate.

After returning from Afghanistan, they intended to settle down and have a family. Their house was full of all sorts of wonderful things they had brought back from their trip.

So when I came back to London from my trip in 1969, it somehow seemed entirely right and natural for me to go and stay with them in their home in Belsize Park, so that is what I did. It was a big house, and although they owned the whole thing, when they had first moved in it was split into flats and they had the top floor. As the other residents either died or moved out, so they reclaimed the flats and turned the place into one wonderful house again.

The rooms were enormous. I remember that the living room, in particular, was huge, and Brenda had a large studio at the back of the house where she would go to paint. And David used to bring the wives of the rich men he drove around back to the house so that Brenda could paint their portraits. It was a nice little earner for them. By this time they had two children, Christopher and Caroline.

CHAPTER 5
BREAKING NEW GROUND

"In my opinion, and the opinion of many others, you are a far better actress than you think you are." - Alan Ayckbourn

So in 1969 I had come back to England from Australia and was living with Brenda and David. My first audition after arriving home was for a new TV series called *Take Three Girls*. They were looking for an upper-class brunette. And here was I – a blonde 'Australian'. I didn't think that I had a hope of landing the part.

Well I must have done something right because I was offered it, and I was delighted to accept. Again though, it was just a job. We had no idea it was going to be a hit series. I wish that I could tell you that I had some kind of crystal ball or that I used to get a feeling in my water that I might have been in at the start of something a bit special but it is not the case. There is no magic formula and there are never any guarantees.

I am sure that some actors and actresses, directors and producers have made TV series and films and have been sure that they have had sure-fire smash hits on their hands, only to watch them disappear into oblivion because that certain something, that little piece of magic, isn't there.

Later in my career I would take parts where I had read the script and was convinced that I was about to appear in a hit, but it would bomb. And you are left scratching your head and wondering why. "I didn't see that coming."

But *Take Three Girls* had everything going for it, and it quickly caught the public's imagination. It was unique because it was the first series on British television that gave the leading roles to women – three of them. It was also the first TV drama series to be screened in colour, which made us all feel like pioneers. It was terrifically exciting.

Take Three Girls was a drama series that focused on the lives of cello-playing Victoria (yours truly), single mother Kate (Susan Jameson) and cockney art student Avril (Angela Down) who shared a flat in London. I had to have cello lessons, not because I was ever going to play on air, but because I had to be convincing when I was pretending to play. They used to bring in a world-famous cellist called Charles Tunnell and when there was a scene in which I was meant to be playing, he would sit behind the camera and do it properly while I mimed the actions. My instrument was fitted with string so that when I played it, it was silent, which may have been a blessing for everybody else in the studio. Subconsciously, I picked up all the mannerisms and I suppose that was because the music was so beautiful and so emotional.

I soon came to realise just how much proper musicians suffer for their art because after I had my cello lessons I had to take it home on the Tube with me so that I could practice – have you ever tried to take a cello onto a packed Underground train? Let me assure you that it is not a simple matter, and everybody stares at you as if you have two heads.

The series was iconic of its time because in real-life London there were so many young women coming to the city and moving into houses and flats with other girls and seeing if they could find what it was that was missing from their lives in the towns and cities where they had come from.

Victoria was a hapless character for whom things were always going wrong, and she was adorable to play. The great James Bolam, who had already made a name for himself with Rodney Bewes in *The Likely Lads*, played my boyfriend in the series. He was already with Susan Jameson and they have been together ever since. Back then they had a rather well known lodger, a young actor by the name of John Thaw.

James is one of the finest actors this country has produced, and yet he is underrated by many people. He always seem to make it look so easy, which is a rare talent. He now stars in *New Tricks* and Alan Armstrong, who is one of his co-stars, is exactly the same – a wonderful actor who hardly ever seems to break sweat. He appeared in *Les Miserables* and stole the show.

The theme tune, *Light Flight* by Pentangle, became a hit in its own right.

The series was split into 12 episodes and each of us headlined four of those. We each had our own writers, our own directors and our own production team, and it made us feel terribly important.

It was a ground-breaking series. I filmed the first series in 1969 alongside Susan Jameson and Angela Down. Susan and I become close friends, and we still are. In many ways it was like doing theatre work as we would rehearse all day and then film it for real in the evening, starting at 8pm and finishing at 10pm. It was like doing it live. Sadly, there is nothing left of any of the series of *Take Three Girls* because the tapes were all wiped.

My sole intention at the time was to earn my fare back to Australia – I had no other thought in my mind.

Back in those days the film industry Down Under was still very much in its infancy and I thought that it would be rather fun to be a part of that, or to go back and do another series for television. The other option was to go and live in Los Angeles – a lot of my Australian friends had gone to LA, and it crossed my mind that it might be a good idea to see if I could crack Hollywood. Anyway, the one thing I was certain of was that I would not be staying in London.

Take Three Girls was hard work. We would rehearse all week and then, finally, production day would arrive and, again, we would rehearse during the day and film each episode between 8pm and 10pm. We had to get it right, and we had to be finished by 10pm because after that we had run out of studio time – there was no way you would get away with saying: "Oh, we just need another five minutes to shoot that scene again." It meant we had to go straight through without any breaks – you may find it difficult to believe but if the episode wasn't finished by 10pm then it was never going to be finished, and the production staff would have had to cobble something together from the film they had in the can. It put added pressure on everybody but, on the other hand, it did ensure that we were all absolutely focused on what we were doing. In effect, every episode took us nine days, with the recording taking two hours right at the end of that process.

There was one episode that still sticks in my mind – it involved a great deal of emotion, and the second we had finished filming it, I burst into tears. I think it was a combination of the emotion of the part and the relief that we had managed to get the thing done properly and on time.

I have always been quite fortunate, however, in as much as by the time I have left a studio or a theatre, I am able to leave the character behind me. The exception to that would be during rehearsal for a new play when you go through this bizarre process of trying to become this new person, and it is not enough to focus on it only when you are in the theatre or the television studio. Becoming a new character is almost like buying new clothes – you keep trying them on until you find something that fits and feels right. But once I have got and the director is happy with it, no I do not take it home.

Some people are unable to do that, and have to live and breathe every part – I have heard of suffering for your art, but I firmly believe that if, for instance, you are called upon to play a drug-taking alcoholic it is not necessary to start popping pills and getting drunk every night to find a way to get into character. There are other, far less stressful and harmful ways of learning.

There is a famous story involving Laurence Olivier, when he was making *Marathon Man* with Dustin Hoffman, and each day Hoffman would arrive on set unshaven and looking as if he hadn't slept all night, because he felt it helped him to get into his character. He explained what he was doing and Olivier said to him: "Dear boy, have you tried acting?"

For me, it is about drawing on life experiences, either my own or those of people I know, and then trying to turn the words on a page into a real person – or as real as a character in a play can ever become, and they certainly need to be believable if you are going to win over an audience.

There have been a number of people who have starred in soaps for many years who eventually find it difficult to tell the difference between the character they play and the person they are meant to be away from the set.

At the end of the first series, I went to Perth theatre in Scotland to work for Joan Knight, who had run Farnham Castle Theatre, where I had worked in the school holidays when I was 14, and before I went to live in Australia. Apart from Perth, she also ran the theatre in Pitlochrie. Joan was a fabulous director, and one of the few women to run a theatre. I performed in a new play by N C Hunter called *One Fair Daughter*, and that was my first experience of touring.

We would get up in the morning, have breakfast, pile into a minibus and head to the next venue, book into a bed and breakfast, do the show, and then repeat the same process all over again. It was a great learning experience. I thought that was what touring was all about, and it came as something of a shock to my system when I later discovered that it wasn't normally like this when you went on tour with a play.

I was in demand and next found myself appearing at the Bristol Old Vic, which was actually in Bath because they were doing up the theatre in Bristol. I appeared in *The Importance of Being Earnest* by Oscar Wilde and *Arms and the Man* by George Bernard Shaw. I appeared in *The Importance of Being Earnest* with Stephen Moore, who has since gone on to become a mainstay of the National Theatre, and Sonia Dresdel played Lady Bracknell. She was a very famous actress in her day, and used to tell stories about actors and actresses getting dressed up to go for lunch at The Ivy, where they would all sit and bitch about their fellow performers before going back to the theatre in the afternoon for a lie down before the evening performance. She was a ferocious character.

The butler was played by the wonderful Simon Cadell, who went on to star in *Hi De Hi*. He was just out of drama school at the time and the two of us teamed up with Hilary Dwyer, who had a car, so all three of us would pile into it and head off out during the day and take in the sights. This would be something that I would come to do on a regular basis while touring with plays.

I mentioned my touring experience in Scotland, where all the accommodation was sorted out for me, and I just assumed it was always like that.

"Well where are we going to be staying then?"

"I have no idea where you are going to be staying Liza – you have to sort that out for yourself."

Back in Bath, I had a room above a pub called The Garrick's Head, which is now offices for the theatre. Breakfast was included and because I wasn't being paid very much for appearing at the Old Vic, I used to eat as much as I possibly could in the morning so that I wouldn't need to eat again for the rest of the day. It sounds ridiculous, but remember that my plan was still to get back to Australia, so I had to watch the pennies.

It was a really exciting time in terms of my work, but there wasn't much time for anything else, and certainly not for boyfriends. Anyway, it felt like I was never in one place long enough to meet young men and spend the time required to establish a relationship. Of course I had the odd date, but there was nobody special at that point. I don't suppose I was particularly interested – I was still trying to establish my career and work out what my next move would be.

Eventually, I returned to make the second series of *Take Three Girls*. Bizarrely, the production team decided to replace Susan and Angela for the second series, and they brought in two actresses, Carolyn Seymour and Barra Grant, who simply were not in the same league as Susan and Angela. I should have said no, and walked away from the series because I knew right away that the chemistry had gone. It is one of these things that I look back on now and say to myself: "Well, I was only 20, and sometimes it is by making mistakes that you learn what it is all about."

I should have gone with my instincts, which were telling me that the

53

magic had disappeared, but I didn't, and it became part of my learning process. To this day, I have no idea why they made the changes they did. They had a series that was hugely successful, and, for no good reason, they changed it and it was gone.

I still had the same script writers, Terence Brady and Charlotte Bingham, so it shouldn't have mattered, but it did. That thing that made it a success had gone. I suppose the producers could have asked Susan and Angela to come back, but it probably wouldn't have worked. Charlotte was a great talent who had written a best-selling novel *Coronet Among the Weeds*, which was about her growing up as a baronet's daughter, and the part I played in *Take Three Girls* was loosely based on Charlotte. Her father was the model for John Le Carre's George Smiley in *Tinker, Tailor, Soldier, Spy*, and her mother was also a writer.

Charlotte is still a brilliant writer who has gone on to produce some wonderful books.

In those days, the script was the most important thing. The BBC took pride in getting together the best writers in the business and commissioning them, and then they would think about who might be cast to play the parts. That art has been lost somewhat. Now what tends to happen is that a big star will be signed up and then they go in search of a suitable script, and I believe that explains in a nutshell why we are served up with so much drivel. The performer, or star if you will, should never be bigger than the show – that is where *Coronation Street* is so terribly clever. Characters become established and viewers regard them as integral parts of the programme and come to believe that they are irreplaceable, but Corrie has proved time and time again that people can come and go and it makes no difference to the quality of the programme. It is all about the scripts and the quality of writing.

Eleven years later, the original cast of *Take Three Girls* were reunited for *Take Three Women* – there were four episodes, shown on BBC2. Victoria was, by then, a widow with a young daughter, Kate had a 13-year-old son and Avril owned an art gallery.

Because *Take Three Girls* was a ground-breaking series and because it was so successful, there was a huge amount of interest from the press, and suddenly I found that I was being recognised whenever I went out. Up until that point, and despite the worldwide success of *Skippy*, I could pretty much go out and about and do whatever I wanted.

Now, there were autograph hunters, and people who just wanted to talk to me because they had seen me on TV. I was intelligent enough to realise that this could have been a fleeting moment in my life, so I always tried to give people time. And the truth is that I quite enjoyed the attention. By now, I also had the money to return to Australia but, for a variety of reasons, it simply never happened.

I probably didn't realise it at the time, but I was incredibly lucky. I'd landed a major role in a TV series in Australia, completed the trip of a lifetime, come back to London and, in no time at all, I had landed a part in highly successful series. This acting business was easy. Or so I thought.

My parents returned to England in 1971, which I suppose ended any lingering thoughts I may have had about going back Down Under. It was good to have them back, and I went to live with them back in Wrecclesham in a house in which Julie Andrews had lived. I worked in various theatres, including the one in Farnham, and was doing pretty nicely.

During that period I went out with a boy called Martin, with whom I had grown up. He might have wanted it to develop into something rather more serious and it might well have done had he not uttered the words: "Once you've got over this acting thing..." That was the end of that relationship. Once I'd got over this 'acting thing'? There may be some individuals who regard it as a character flaw to want to be other people all the time, but it was, and is, what got my adrenalin going. I simply love dressing up and pretending to be somebody else – not that I have any problems about being myself you understand.

I get a script and when I start to read it I pretty much straight away form an idea in my head as to how I intend to play it, but sometimes you can be blown out the water by a director or writer who has an entirely different image in his mind. And at the end of the day, if a writer tells you that he wants you to play a role in a specific way, then who am I to argue with him? It is his creation after all.

Later in my career I would go on to do quite a bit of work for Alan Ayckbourn and, with him, I would never have any preconceived ideas because I learnt at a fairly early stage that I was usually way off beam when I imagined how he would want me to interpret his characters. When he writes, he has a very specific idea in his mind about his plays and the individuals he has created, and you simply have to respect that.

Alan always sits me down and tells me what his creations are thinking, and I learnt at a very early stage to make notes of everything he said to me, and then I would go away and read it back and realise that he had given me a complete blueprint for what he wanted me to do. But he would do it without actually telling me what to do. Genius.

He is an amazing man. He used to type his plays with two fingers, but then he suffered a stroke and, for a time, thought that he might never work again, but he is a determined individual and he battled back and is still writing, even though he now types with just one finger. It is quite, quite extraordinary. The body may not be what it was, but his brain remains as sharp as ever.

Alan is twice as prolific as Shakespeare was and what he does with his writing is to chronicle our times so that in 100 years' time, a theatre company will be able to pick up a script and know precisely what life was like in 20th and 21st century Britain. He started writing in the 1950s, and all of his plays are of the time. Although the settings and the eras may change, people's emotions remain the same – it's just that they wear slightly different clothes. Like Oscar Wilde, he is capable of saying as much with one funny line as another author might do in two pages of speech to make the same point. All of Alan's plays have tremendous depth.

I will return to my relationship with Alan later and in some depth because he has been so important in both my life and my career.

Back in 1971, my parents had returned to England and I am sure that Dad thought he could walk straight back into his old job at the BBC. Of course, that was never a possibility. They would offer him a job, but it would be several notches below the level he had been at before. He was a very proud man, and refused to do that. The result was that he became very withdrawn and began to suffer from depression.

Then, out of the blue, he was asked if he was interested in setting up a new series that was to be called *Emmerdale Farm*, so off he went to Yorkshire. Right from the start, the series he had in his mind was a televised version of The Archers, and that was more or less exactly as it turned out. His idea was that the series would revolve around the farming seasons, and it quickly captured people's imagination and picked up a sizeable following.

I don't think he ever dreamt that it would be as successful as it went on to become – and he would have laughed out loud if you had told him that, all these years later, it would still be going strong. It has, of course, been renamed *Emmerdale* and in many ways it has been rebranded.

Now it is a TV soap set in the Yorkshire Dales and one of the characters just so happens to be a farmer. But the farm is no longer the central theme of the series. It had to move with the times or else it would have just withered and died. Any series that survives for a length of time does so because it is regularly infused with new blood and fresh ideas.

Dad was more or less living in Leeds full-time, while Mum remained in Farnham. She could have moved up north with him but chose not to. I was surprised that they had remained together for as long as they did but in 1974 they eventually did split up and were divorced. In all honesty their marriage should have ended many years before it did as they seemed to fight all the time and the atmosphere at home was not pleasant.

At that point, my mother decided there was nothing to keep her in England so she took Maria and returned to Australia, settling in Perth, which is probably the most isolated city on the planet.

Dad then met and got together with a woman called Pam, with whom he had my half-brother, William. So you can see that my family life was quite complicated. Dad eventually returned with Pam to Putney before they ended up moving to the Lake District. They finally settled in Cornwall. My grandparents had a house in Cornwall, and we had spent all our childhood holidays there, as had my father before me. The coastline is truly spectacular, with views that take your breath away.

I do, however, remember it being cold and wet for most of them time, and being forced to spend time on the beach regardless of the weather. We would go for the most enormous walks before breakfast, and then have a picnic on the beach – rain, hail or shine.

As my career developed, my father was always quick to praise me, but I could never win the approval of my mother and the result was that I never felt good enough for her. The best I ever got from her was: "Yes, you were all right, I suppose." It hardly made me feel special, and it made me determined that if ever I had children of my own I would go out of my way to encourage them in whatever path they chose to follow, and I would praise them in their endeavours.

Love is a special thing, and it means a great deal to know that somebody loves you and wants you to do well in your life – I always had that feeling from my father. Because of my mother and the way she made me feel, there were definitely times in my life when I did not strive to achieve things in the way that I should have done, when I felt that I really wasn't quite good enough.

Alan Ayckbourn gave me a card in 2010, inside which he had written the following words: "In my opinion, and the opinion of many others, you are a far better actress than you think you are." It made me cry, and I now take it everywhere with me because it meant so much to me. But I was shocked to think that at the age of 60, people could still see that I suffered from feelings of inadequacy.

Meanwhile back in my career, *Take Three Girls* came to an end, but I wasn't worried. I had gone from one job to another so far in my career and I was convinced that I would do the same thing again. Still I kept hearing stories about actors who spent most of their lives out of work, but that wasn't my experience. And, sure enough, there would be another major television part for me, but not before I had spent some time working in the theatre with some of the very best performers.

When the second series finished, I headed back to Perth to appear in another N C Hunter play and found that my co-star was none other than Tom Fleming, who had played Jesus way back in the 1950s when I had been required to sit on his knee. Now, here I was playing his mistress.

CHAPTER 6
TREADING THE BOARDS

"No no darling. I am not wearing that – I will look like a fire hydrant and dogs will piss on me. I want black." - Coral Brown

In 1972 I had been offered a part in *Lady Windermere's Fan*, written by Oscar Wilde. It was part of the BBC's Play of the Month series that ran from 1965 until 1983, and I relished the prospect of appearing in it alongside the likes of Sian Phillips, Coral Brown, Ronald Hines, Derek Godfrey, Judy Geeson and Charles Gray. Play of the Month was a fabulous way of introducing television audiences to plays that would normally only be performed in theatres. It was an inspired concept because it whetted the appetite of millions of people who had never considered going to the theatre before.

I believe it was a mistake to scrap it. The great thing about it was it also gave television exposure to actors and actresses who spent most of their lives working in the theatre.

Lady Windermere's Fan was an incredible production. Coral and Sian used to have competitions to see who could wear the best and most exclusive clothes to work, so one day Sian would turn up clothed from head to toe in Yves St Laurent while Coral, who went on to marry

Vincent Price, would be in a Chanel outfit. Every single day they would arrive for rehearsals in different outfits, with matching shoes, handbags and hats. They always looked sensational and the rest of the cast used to have fun wondering what outfits they would be wearing each day. Coral was born in Melbourne and was a typically outspoken Australian.

Cecil Beaton designed the costumes for the show and one day he showed Coral a design for a gorgeous red dress. She took one look at it and said: "No no darling. I am not wearing that – I will look like a fire hydrant and dogs will piss on me. I want black." And she got black. She was an outrageous character, but a great actress. In 1958 she went to Russia with the Royal Shakespeare Company and while she was there she met Guy Burgess, the spy. That meeting was the basis for Alan Bennett's play *An Englishman Abroad*.

Twenty years later I was asked to appear in *An Englishman Abroad*, which gave me the chance to play Coral Brown, and of course I had this clear image in my mind of how she looked, behaved and dressed. Robert Powell played Guy Burgess.

Lady Windermere's Fan was a terrific experience for a young actress, but 1972 turned out to be a landmark year for me in other ways, as I also got to work with a genius, one of several I have been fortunate enough to share my working life with.

Sadly, many of today's generation will not have the faintest idea who I am talking about when I mention Dick Emery, who was one of Britain's greatest comic actors and comedians. I was lucky enough to appear with him in the film *Ooh, You are Awful* – nobody would ever claim that it was a classic, but it was good fun and everybody involved with it had a great time filming it. I also worked with him on television, which was how I landed the part in the movie, which was directed by Cliff Owen, who was a very influential director who also worked with Peter Sellers and Morecambe and Wise.

Many big stars are monsters, but Dick was divine. Yes, he was very naughty, rude and outrageous, but he didn't have a nasty bone in his body.

The plot went something like this:

Near the start of the film, conmen Charlie Tully (Emery) and Reggie Peek have successfully conned two Italian men, and are making an easy escape with £500,000. Flushed with success, Tully is unable to resist running a 'quick and easy' minor con on a passing American tourist. But the 'quick and easy' con unexpectedly goes awry, and Tully is arrested. Peek escapes and deposits the £500,000 in a bank in Switzerland, while Tully is sent to prison. Time passes, and when Tully is released, he is met by Peek, who intends to tell him the bank account number. But their reunion is cut short when Peek is murdered, on the orders of London crime lord Sid Sabbath, with whose girlfriend Peek has been having an affair.

Peek has left a record of the bank account number, but in an unusual way. Befitting his reputation as a womaniser, the digits are tattooed on the bottoms of four young women. Tully adopts a range of disguises, to track down each woman in turn and see her bottom. Meanwhile, Tully's antics are being followed by other - more dangerous - criminals: one group from London, and another from Rome.

The first woman he finds is a British Rail announcer, who disrobes inside a photo booth at Waterloo station.

The second is a bride on her wedding day, who is exposed before all her guests.

Number three is Liza Missenden Green, the daughter of a peer (played by me), who Tully peeks at through her bedroom window.

Last in the list is a policewoman at a police training school, so Tully enters the school, disguised as a trainee WPC. After a scene in which he spies on a multitude of nubile young recruits, he discovers the digits during a physical training session.

On various occasions, Tully is confronted by members of Sid Sabbath's gang, with orders to do to him as they did to Peek - only for them to mysteriously die themselves. Tully thinks he is 'lucky', Sabbath thinks Tully is a one-man army, and neither realise Tully is actually being guarded by Italian gangsters lurking in the background. The two Italian men conned at the start of the movie had Mafia connections - a 'Godfather' has ordered Tully be kept safe until he can be brought to Rome...

My big scene involved Dick's character peeking through a window at me and although the film was a comedy, I had no clothes on and I was quite nervous about the whole thing, so it was a closed set – only people who had to be there were allowed. I had to get into one of those keep fit contraptions that involved a vibrating rubber belt, and it was extremely undignified. It was the one and only nude scene that I ever did. I vowed there and then that I would never do another. It was a horrible, embarrassing experience, so much so that one of the other girls refused to do it, so they had to get a body double for her.

The only reason that I agreed to do the scene was because I knew that Cliff Owen was a good director and I thought that if I did what he asked then it might lead on to other movie parts with him, but it never did. It was another lesson for me: never do a job hoping that it will lead to other things. Life is not like that. Do each job for the sake of the job.

Of course Emery was the star of the film – it was a vehicle for his talents after all. But that did not prevent him being incredibly kind and generous with the rest of the cast, who included Ronald Fraser, Pat Coombs, William Franklyn and Cheryl Kennedy.

Many comedians have reputations for being maudlin off stage, but not Emery. He was a laugh a minute. I have worked with a lot of comedians and have always been fortunate to have come across men who have been as funny in real life as they were while performing. Some of them may well go home and sit under a black cloud, but I have never seen any evidence of it, and certainly not with Dick.

When you think about it, it must be a heck of a strain to spend your whole life trying to make people laugh, but the likes of Les Dawson, Tommy Cooper and Ken Dodd were able to do so without uttering a word, and Dick could do that too, especially with some of the characters he created – a raised eyebrow, a wink or a trip would be enough. And he never went over the top. He knew exactly how far to go.

He also had a wealth of jokes upon which he could call, so if ever we were sitting around and there was a lull in the conversation, Dick would just start reeling off the jokes.

So I was barely out of my teens, and I had already worked with Coral Brown and Dick Emery. Life couldn't get much better. Except that it did...

A lot of people think that David Jason got his first big break as the hapless shop boy in *Open all Hours*, with Ronnie Barker. But he had been around for a long time before that. For a start, he starred in a brilliant children's TV series called *Do Not Adjust Your Set* alongside a great comedy actress called Denise Coffey. It was Monty Python for children.

I first came across Jason in 1972 when we both appeared in *No Sex Please, We're British*. It was obvious right from the start that this man was a genius. I have been incredibly fortunate to have worked with so many people who were right at the top of the tree, but Jason was in a class of his own when it came to comedy and timing.

I landed the part because I had done *Take Three Girls* and was regarded as being a 'name', somebody who would guarantee bums on seats.

Prior to this I had done a play in the West End called *Signs of the Times*, starring alongside the incomparable Kenneth More, who played Douglas Bader in *Reach for the Sky*, and Norman Beaton, who was this country's first really famous black actor. There is now a Norman Beaton prize for drama students, but he would be laughing in his grave to know that there was now an award named after him because he was an outrageous character. He would have women turning up at the theatre, child in one hand, hanky in the other to dab the tears that ran down their cheeks.

On one occasion the police turned up to arrest Norman, and Kenneth said: "Would you mind awfully arresting him after the show, please? It's just that we have a full house, and I don't know how on earth we would explain his absence."

"Yes, okay Mr More."

He arrived on another occasion, complaining that the bailiffs had been in his flat and had boarded it up so that he couldn't get in. He was a wonderful character, but outrageous with it.

Another night he announced that he was going to cook for us and ended up making pigs' tail soup. None of us had ever heard of such a concoction, but this was true Caribbean food, and it was divine.

Kenneth was just heavenly. He always played the part of the good guy, and I am sure that people must have thought it was impossible that he really be that person in real life, but I am here to tell you that he was.

Kenneth More was an angel, an absolute joy to work with, and a delight to be with.

I knew that I was in the presence of a legend. He was married to Angela Douglas and they had an amazing house in Holland Park that he bought with the money he was paid for making *Reach for the Sky*. As one of Britain's leading actors, he was very well paid.

In those days, people who worked in the West End also earned a fortune. You have to remember that back in the 1950s and '60s, very little money was spent on advertising, so the theatres could afford to look after the stars. Nowadays, when a new play or musical is released, they will spend £1m on promoting it without batting an eyelid, and that means the performers earn less than you might think they do.

Don't go feeling sorry for us though, because leading actors and actresses in top West End shows still do very, very well, thank you very much. And nobody would complain about the sums of money spent on promoting a show because without the promotion and the advertising, there would be no show. Word of mouth is no longer enough.

The play with Kenneth More sold out every night because people wanted to see him in the flesh, having watched him in so many great British movies.

As it turned out, John Gale, the producer, was also involved in staging *No Sex Please, We're British*, and recommended me for a part in that too. I was on cloud nine. If I had been asked to sit down and write how I would want the early part of my acting career to develop, this is the way it would have been. I could scarcely believe my luck, especially as you hear so many stories about promising young actors and actresses who end up giving up on their dreams because they can't land a decent role.

No Sex Please was already running, with David Jason taking over from

Michael Crawford, who was and remains another comic genius. It was a brilliant show, and David took to it like a duck to water. I wouldn't have thought it would be possible for anybody to be better than Crawford, but David was, especially with the physical stuff.

There was one gag that he used to perform every night that involved him unwrapping a parcel covered in brown paper, and he would put the paper, shiny side down, on the side of the stage. The scene would carry on and everybody would forget it was there but, every night, he did this thing where he would deliberately slip on the brown paper and slide all the way across the front of the stage while still standing on the paper. When he came to a standstill he would take a bow to the audience, and then he would fall over. It brought the house down every night, and each time I watched him perform the stunt I was in awe of him because it never once went wrong.

He was absolutely focused on getting it right because, like the rest of us, he loved getting laughs, and revelled in entertaining the audience.

The Strand Theatre held 2,000 people and it was packed out every single night – sometimes the show would over-run by as much as twenty minutes because the audience would laugh so much, and we would have to stand on stage and wait for them to stop before we could carry on with the next line. It was incredible.

I played the straight role, and worked hard at feeding David his lines properly. He used to say that if I did this and he did that, then he was certain we would get a bigger laugh. And do you know what? He got it right every single time. Right up until his final performance, David was always working to try and improve things.

He also used to try and make me laugh when I wasn't supposed to. For instance, when he came on stage I would never know what he was going to be wearing, whether it be daft wigs or even a crash helmet.

Clint Eastwood once said: "Take the work seriously, but not yourself," and David Jason was the perfect example of that. It also applies to each and every one of the greatest actors that I have worked with – they do not disappear up their own backsides. To make comedy work, you have to take it seriously because the moment you start taking it for granted and stop working at it is the moment when the laughter will stop.

The truth is that you are only ever as good as your last script. There have been some genius performers who could read out the crossword clues and make them sound wonderful, but that gift is endowed to a tiny minority. People have said that I am a good comedy actress and while I accept that I bring a certain amount of talent and experience to each part, without a good script I would be lost at sea.

I learnt a huge amount about comedy acting from David, but *No Sex Please* was hard work – we would do a matinee and then an evening performance, at the end of which we would all be dripping in sweat because of all the running around we had to do, but it was a joy and because of David, it felt like we were doing a different show every time we went out on stage.

Jean Kent played the maternal role. She was a formidable woman, quite scary really if you were a young actor. When Jean left the show she was replaced by the incredible Maureen O'Sullivan, who was Mia Farrow's mother. Maureen was a delightfully dippy soul who loved to suck a Fisherman's Friend before she went on. Just before she got her cue, she would remove it from her move and put it down on the struts at the side of the stage, the result being that the struts were covered in old Fisherman's Friends – I don't think anybody could face clearing them away.

She went on *Desert Island Discs* and was asked what her luxury item would be. Quick as a flash she replied: "Valium." She was a divine individual but was completely loopy.

CHAPTER 7
YES HONESTLY

"When I read the scripts for each episode I knew that I was reading something special. They made me laugh out loud – every single time. They were incredibly well crafted."

In 1974, there was a comedy series called *No Honestly*, which starred husband and wife team John Alderton and Pauline Collins. It was a huge success but it only lasted for 13 episodes, spread over two series, because John and Pauline were not interested in continuing – they had enjoyed it while it lasted but wanted to move on to other things.

My next big television part was just around the corner, and once again, it was more or less handed to me on a plate.

Towards the end of 1974, I was asked to appear in a follow-up to the Alderton-Collins series, called *Yes, Honestly*, and I ended up being cast alongside Donal Donnelly and Georgina Melville. I played a character called Lily Pond Browne – well it was a comedy. It was directed by John Bingham and was written by Charlotte Bingham and Terence Brady, who also wrote *No, Honestly*, and it ran for 26 episodes.

Donal played Matthew Browne, a struggling musician, who hires a secretary played by yours truly, they fall in love and eventually get married. As has happened to me so many times during my career, I was presented with brilliant scripts by Charlotte and Terence, and I loved the programme, which went out on ITV.

Donal, who was Irish, was one of life's eccentrics, and he took himself off to New York after we had finished filming and ended up appearing on Broadway and loving every single minute of it. He was larger than life.

The episodes would start with our characters sat on stools talking to one another, and we would then do the story, and it would end with us sitting on the stools again. The scripts were marvellous and I seemed to spend half my time laughing hysterically with Donal, who was just fabulous company, a joy to be with.

Sometimes you can pick up a script and read it from cover to cover and you find yourself wondering whether it will work, whether people will enjoy it. When I read the scripts for each episode of *Yes, Honestly*, I knew that I was reading something special. They made me laugh out loud – every single time. They were incredibly well crafted. It was no surprise because both Terence and Charlotte were very funny people anyway.

Each episode was filmed in front of a live audience, which was fabulous because you knew instantly whether or not the gags were working. I don't mind telling you that this was also a role that was very well paid. I had heard all these stories about young actors and actresses who spent months, and even years, between jobs, and who were forced to do whatever it took to keep the wolf from the door.

When I had arrived in England from Australia, it was always part of my plan to head back Down Under because I had loved my life there so much. There were nothing but good memories really. The idea was to do some work here and earn enough money to pay for my flight back to

Australia.

What actually happened was that I found myself in demand, working almost non-stop for a good number of years, and being paid for doing what I had always wanted to do. And then, of course, my parents returned to Britain and part of my reason for going back had disappeared.

Apart from my appearance, I became best known for my voice, which I suppose lends itself to playing well-to-do characters. I get asked if I had to work at it, or whether I had elocution lessons but the truth is that I didn't. This was the voice that I was born with – I sound very much like my father did. I can do quite a few accents, but I struggle with Liverpool and Geordie for some reason.

CHAPTER 8
AND BABY MAKES TWO

"Having Thom changed my life and got me back on the rails. He gave me something to focus on other than myself. It was a period when I could quite easily have hit the bottle or started taking drugs."

While I had been working in *No Sex Please*, I got involved in a relationship that should never have started, but resulted in me falling pregnant with my son Thom. There are some things in life that are best left unsaid, and the identity of Thom's father is one of those things. Suffice to say that the relationship was one of the biggest mistakes of my life.

I found myself asking: "Liza, what on earth did you do that for?" My parents had divorced, my sister Maria had nearly died with anorexia, my father was living and working in Yorkshire, and my mother had taken Maria to live in West Australia, so it was a pretty bleak period in my personal life – it seemed to me that, in an instant, everybody I had loved had abandoned me and I was left to my own devices.

I felt lonely and I suppose it was kind of inevitable that I would end up in a bad relationship and finish up getting myself pregnant and having a baby. I don't remember thinking it at the time, but when I look back on it now, I believe I probably got pregnant because I thought that having a baby to look after would make everything in my life all right again.

The relationship with Thom's father was one that I knew could never go anywhere because he wasn't right for me. I could have had an abortion or I could have had Thom adopted, and nobody would ever have known, but neither of those options ever entered my head. In the end, having Thom changed my life and got me back on the rails. He gave me something to focus on other than myself. I managed to shake myself out of the frame of mind I was in and I began to count my blessings and realise just how lucky I was. I will always be grateful to my son for that, even though he couldn't possibly have known it. He was a beautiful baby, absolutely enchanting.

It was 1976 and I had just landed a part in a series called *The Brothers*, which was one of the most successful that the BBC ever produced. I suppose you would describe it as a British equivalent of *Dallas*. It ran for four years, and remained as fresh at the end as it was when it began, and it was compulsive viewing. Please don't think I am blowing my own trumpet here, because I am not. I did not appear in it from the start, and it was already an established favourite by the time I arrived on the scene.

The series featured the Hammond family, which ran a transport firm called Hammond Transport Services. It began just after the death of patriarch and founder Robert Hammond. The eldest son, Edward prepared to take over the running of the firm and then discovers that his father had left equal shares of the business to his two other sons, Brian (played by Richard Easton) and David (Robin Chadwick) and to his mistress and secretary Jennifer Kingsley (Jennifer Wilson).

It was a story of family conflict, driven by the fact that Brian and David really were not suited to running and expanding the company. Just to add some spice to the plot, there was also a romance between Edward and Jennifer. One of the oddities of the series was that initially Edward was played by Glyn Owen, who was replaced by Patrick O'Connell after the end of the first series.

There was plenty of love interest, and glamour provided by David's girlfriend Jill (Gabrielle Drake). They also found a villain of the piece in Colin Baker who played a financial whiz kid called Paul Merroney – if you think of Michael Douglas in the movie *Wall Street*, you will not be too far off the mark. I came into the series as his wife, April Winter. And then there was the wonderful Kate O'Mara, who played the boss of an air freight business.

Another key character was Bill, the foreman, played by Derek Benfield. In many ways, *The Brothers* reflected what was actually happening in the workplace in Britain at the time. Benfield's character found himself being promoted from the shop floor to become a key member of the board, and the resistance with which that role was met was pretty indicative of what was happening elsewhere. There was one episode when the script came in and for reasons that nobody could ever fathom, his character's name had been changed to Ruby, and so he became known as Ruby after that.

The show also featured Mike Pratt in the role of Don Stacey, which turned out to be the last part he played before his death.

The matriarch was played by a fabulous actress called Jean Anderson, who also acted as a mother figure to the cast when the cameras stopped rolling. She was a very gracious woman and the relationship she had with Richard Easton, her son in the series, was actually like a real-life mother and son. She was always immaculately dressed, and every day she and Richard would sit down together and do the *Telegraph* crossword.

I made my appearance at the end of the sixth series and was heavily pregnant at the time, so I had to wear a big fur coat in order to hide the bump. By the time filming for the seventh series began I'd had Thom (he was born in April 1976) – in fact, I was back at work just six weeks after having him. My mother also returned from Australia and bought a house that she had made into two flats, so Thom and I moved in with her and she helped to look after the baby while I was filming.

The programme went out on a Sunday, and it became so popular that evening church services were moved in order that people could get home to watch it. When God is asked to stand aside, you know that you are appearing in something important.

I can honestly say that it was a delight to be a part of that programme. The cast were all incredibly friendly and we had lots of laughs together. In those days there were purpose-built rehearsal rooms in Acton – it was a big building and we were sharing it with performers from lots of other programmes. The canteen was on the top floor and when we went for lunch you could find yourself having lunch with Dr Who (Jon Pertwee in those days), Bruce Forsyth, a cyberman, dancing girls or a Roman soldier. And we just took it all for granted, but it was a quite extraordinary and blissful part of my life.

A group of actors were rehearsing for a series called *Wings*, set during the Second World War, and they got into the habit of playing cricket indoors, in their rehearsal room. It was a vast room, ideal for the purpose really, but the problem was that they played so much cricket that they left skid marks from the cricket balls all over the floor.

We would rehearse for ten days and then the entire cast would head up to Birmingham's Pebble Mill studios to film each episode. The series was filmed during the summer, and one of my abiding memories was of how hot it was. Every day the sun beat down upon us. It was glorious, except for the fact that the rehearsal studios had huge glass windows and there was no air conditioning, so you can imagine how hot they became. It was like working in a sauna.

At the end of the seventh series, we were told: "Okay guys, thanks for that. It's been a great run and we will see you next year for series eight."

I headed off for home feeling pretty pleased with myself for having landed a part in a series that had become such a phenomenon, and I waited for the letter or call to tell me to come back and start work on series eight. Except that there was no series eight. It was the strangest thing because at no stage did anybody ever make the announcement that the show had come to an end.

The strangest thing of all was that it was still as popular as it had ever been. People loved it. I am sure that there must have been a very good reason for scrapping it, but I was never able to work out what it was. Maybe they simply wanted to go out on a high. All too often, series go on too long, outstay their welcome and just kind of dribble away into oblivion. When that happens, you get a feeling that it is about to come to an end, but nobody sensed that with this one.

Nobody could ever say that about *The Brothers*, and I was genuinely sad that it finished, not least because apart from appearing in such an iconic series, I was earning good money and could afford to enjoy a decent lifestyle.

And speaking of lifestyle, *The Brothers* was a case of real life reflecting art in more ways than one. Colin Baker and I were attracted to one another pretty much from the first time that we met one another. He was good looking, charming and he made me laugh, and before we knew where we were, the two of us were in a relationship. We had fallen in love with one another.

I tended to leap into things back then without thinking about the consequences – I still do it now to a certain extent. Our relationship seemed like a good idea at the time, and when he asked me to marry him, well of course I said yes. From meeting to getting married all happened in a matter of months. We had a huge do at the Savoy hotel in London, attended by all the cast members from *The Brothers*. Colin had a lovely flat in Hampstead where we lived for a while, and then we decided that we wanted to live in the country so we looked around and ended up buying a house in Oxfordshire. I was unhappy almost from the day that we moved in, and I began to get this uneasy feeling that I had made a huge mistake in marrying Colin.

Then we went on tour in a truly dreadful play. So we were performing in the evening in something that we both knew was awful and we weren't happy during the day. We began to bicker and grow apart.

To make matters worse, we had Thom with us – he was a young baby and he seemed to be ill all the time, so that simply added to the strain. Naturally, I spent most of my time worrying about him. I went from doctor to doctor, hospital to hospital and they kept telling me that I was neurotic and that were absolutely nothing wrong with my 18-month-old son, but I knew that there was. One doctor even suggested to me that I should take tranquillisers. I wanted to throttle him. "Right then, so being dotty is the reason Thom has diarrhoea and is being sick all the time, is it?"

Finally I took Thom to a paediatrician who was prepared to take me seriously and told me that my son was lactose intolerant and I should take him off all dairy products. Guess what? Within 24 hours he was completely better. He had been projectile vomiting prior to that. Anyway, I had confirmation of something I already knew – that I was in no way neurotic. I was simply a mother who had been desperately worried about her child.

As much of a relief as it was to have Thom well again, it did nothing to repair my ever deteriorating relationship with Colin. I was learning to my cost that we should have remained as friends because, as things turned out, we were not compatible. There was no specific reason for our relationship falling apart. It didn't help that we were both busy actors, which meant that we spent a good deal of time apart from one another. That should have made the time we spent together extra special; instead, we found that we were bickering. Marriage ruined a very fine friendship.

I was deeply unhappy and ended up bolting because I knew that I had to get out the relationship. There was nobody else involved; I know people always say that, but it was true. Neither of us was seeing anybody else.

From start to finish, we were together for about two years, from 1977 until 1979. It had all seemed such a good idea at the time. It was a blessing that we were able to recognise so early that it would never work out. I think that after having Thom, perhaps I was looking for somebody who could look after the two of us.

Our parting was fairly acrimonious and it was a long time before we started talking again, but I am pleased to say that I now regard him as a friend. You will not hear me saying a word against him. Colin is a great actor, a very fine fellow and excellent company, but we were not right for each other. He deserved better.

He remarried to a woman who was perfectly suited to him, and they went on to have four beautiful daughters, and he is very happy now. I would eventually find my perfect partner too, but not before another mistake or two along the way.

Funnily enough, we worked together in a production of *She Stoops to Conquer* in 2007, playing a married couple. We hadn't had much contact with one another over the years but within a couple of days, the friendship we'd had all those years earlier was re-established. It made me realise how much I like him, and reinforced my view that we should have remained as friends.

After our divorce, I had enough money to put down a deposit on a house in Muswell Hill.

CHAPTER 9
HOME SWEET HOME

"I landed a part in a TV comedy called Watch This Space. It wasn't vintage comedy – in fact it was terrible. But I don't think I have ever laughed as much in my entire life as I did while making that series."

One of my abiding memories of my house is Muswell Hill was what the previous owner had done to the walls of the sitting room. They had applied what looked like flock wallpaper, which would have been bad enough, but this was much worse. A type of glue had been applied to the walls and this awful green fibre glass-like substance was put on top of that.

When I went to view the house, the vendor proudly show me this hideous wall and announced that he had lots more of it, and that I could do the rest of the house with it. He had been going to do it himself, he said, but sadly he hadn't had time. He had bright red, orange, yellow, blue. What a shame!

Getting it up was bad enough, but removing it was well-nigh impossible. It would have been easier to have knocked the walls down! The surface was like action man's head. I tried to burn in off but that gave off noxious fumes and then I tried to scrape it off, but made no impression on it whatsoever. In the end, I got a builder in and asked him to plaster over it.

I was very happy at that time in my life, helped by the fact that I was doing lots of TV work. My mother had returned from Australia and throughout period she was a rock when it came to helping me to look after Thom. She even moved in with me in Muswell Hill. It was great because it meant that I could go to work and not worry about him.

I landed a part in a TV comedy called *Watch this Space*, set in an advertising agency. It also starred Christopher Biggins, Gillian Taylforth, Peter Blake and Linda Bellingham and it was joyous – I don't think I have ever laughed as much in my entire life as I did while making that series. It wasn't vintage comedy. In fact, it was terrible, but I got on like a house on fire with the rest of the cast, and we all just used to spark off one another.

I was not keen to leave Thom with a nanny, but leaving him with his grandmother was a different matter altogether. It is very difficult to combine the roles of mother of a young child with being an actress. If you are lucky enough to be part of a television series then it is great because you generally know precisely what your routine is going to be. You know what time you have to leave the house in the morning, what time you will get home and what days you will have to work, and you can organise your life around that. While I was filming *The Brothers*, that is precisely what happened.

But if you are a jobbing actress and you have to tour the country with a play, it is a very different kettle of fish, and it can leave you with some tough decisions to make. If your child is of school age, then you have no choice – if you are a single mother, as I was, then you have to rely on family or, if that is not possible, you need to employ the services of a nanny to look after your child. And that creates its own set of problems.

How do you feel about leaving your son or daughter with somebody who is a complete stranger? Will she look after them in the same way that you would? Will she end up taking over your role as a mother?

If your son or daughter is not at school, you still face tough decisions. Yes, you may be able to look after him or her during the day, although not always because there is rehearsal time and there are matinees. Do you ask a family member to go on tour with you so that they can look after the child when you are on stage? Or, again, do you hire a nanny?

So you will understand why I so grateful to my mother for taking all that stress and worry out of my life. At that time my sister was living in California, having married an American. They lived in Monterey and Mum would sometimes take Thom there and stay with my sister. At that time, Monterey was exactly as described by John Steinbeck in *Cannery Row*, which was set on a street in the town lined with sardine fisheries.

It still boasted the old train tracks and boilers, and the canneries were still there. It has all changed now, of course. Permission was sought to build hotels and suchlike on the land where the canneries stood and when that permission was denied, mysteriously, the canneries caught fire and were burnt to the ground – to be replaced by hotels. The train tracks were lifted, and a running track and giant aquarium were built and it became a tourist trap.

But in the days when Mum took Thom to Monterey, Clint Eastwood was the mayor of Carmel and he had a bar called The Hog's Breath and he would regularly be seen in there having a drink. I used to spend a lot of holiday time there, and it seemed totally bizarre to be able to walk past this legendary Hollywood figure and to be able to say: "Hi Clint, how are you doing?" He was a real down to earth man. Despite all the success he had achieved, he cared deeply about the area, and he was perfectly happy to talk to complete strangers, people who were in awe of his very presence.

It was around this time that I met David Cobham for the first time – he was to cast me in *Brendon Chase*. David was a renowned director, especially when it came to the natural world, and I began to work with him on a regular basis. He was 20 years older than me and although I didn't know it at the time, he would come to play a huge part in both my professional and my private life.

CHAPTER 10
DENNIS THE MENACE

"If George was quiet and reserved, Dennis was exactly the opposite. Minder was being made when he was going through his wild spell – he could never be accused of not enjoying life to the full."

At the end of the 1970s and into the early 1980s, I was working almost non-stop, doing lots of television work.

I did lots of one-off programmes, such as *Going for a Song* with the adorable Arthur Neagus and Robert Robinson (it was one of the first antique shows and it got the public hooked), *Basil Brush* (it was very strange having dialogue with what amounted to a glove puppet), *Whodunnit?*, *Crown Court*, *Wodehouse Playhouse*, *Cannon and Ball* (two very funny men), *Blankety Blank* (Les Dawson and Terry Wogan were a scream) and my first appearance on *Give us a Clue* (more of that later).

As an actor, you get to do some roles that are fun from start to finish and you get other parts that are sheer hard work and bring you little enjoyment from beginning to end. The episode of *Minder* that I did most definitely falls into the former category.

It was a hugely popular series in which George Cole played Arthur Daley, a dodgy car dealer with his finger in many pies, and Dennis

Waterman as Terry, his faithful sidekick and the 'minder' of the title. Most stories followed the same pattern, with Arthur coming up with a sure-fire money-making scheme that you knew was going to end in tears for somebody, usually Terry.

My episode involved a racehorse scam, and I played the part of a jockey, which was hardly a hardship to me anyway. It involved a scene in which my character was taking part in a race and I was lining up at the start on top of a magnificent – and very powerful - horse, and all the jockeys, who were professional riders, kept goading me: "Go on Liza, you'd love to go over the jumps, wouldn't you?"

"No, I wouldn't!"

"Aw, go on, go on. You know you want to."

"I do not want to. It's dangerous."

"But you are a proper rider. You can do it, of course you can."

Jockeys are a nightmare, full of fun, but with a wicked sense of humour. The producers had got a double in to do the jumps for me because even if I had wanted to do them myself, the insurance company wouldn't allow it.

George Cole was a lovely, quiet man who, in the evenings used to like to go off and have dinner on his own. He was always very polite, genuine and warm, but nothing like the character he played. I went on to work with his daughter, Tara, who is a brilliant costume supervisor. His wife, Penny, is also a delightful woman.

Although George was not gregarious, he was very funny.

If George was quiet and reserved, Dennis was exactly the opposite. *Minder* was being made when he was going through his wild spell – he could never be accused of not enjoying life to the full, and why not? He had already established himself as a big star when appearing as John

Thaw's sidekick in *The Sweeney*, the gritty series about life in the Flying Squad.

He was, and is, a tremendous actor who thoroughly enjoyed a good laugh, he oozed charisma and the girls thought he was fabulous. He smoked and he enjoyed a drink but once he got on set he was professionalism personified. How he had the energy to pack it all in I simply don't know.

In his prime he came across as a naughty boy, and women loved that in him. He still has a special kind of magnetism – it is the sort of thing that is difficult to put your finger on, but there are a few people who possess it.

Even in *New Tricks*, in which he plays a retired policeman, he is still the member of the team that you would regard as being the 'naughty boy', so it is entirely believable when he breaks the rules and goes off and does his own thing in the series without telling his boss Sandra Pullman (played by Amanda Redman). Of course, it helps that James Bolam and Alun Armstrong complete what is a very, very strong cast, all of whom bring something unique to the show.

CHAPTER 11
HURRAY FOR HOLLYWOOD!

"Now the thing is Liza, we want you to play it as an American. Do you think that you can handle that honey?"

Two significant episodes in my life happened in 1980. First of all, I was offered the part of Nellie Bligh in a comedy called *Pig in the Middle*. I had enjoyed success in *Yes, Honestly* and the new series was written by Terence Brady and Charlotte Bingham, who had also created *Yes, Honestly*.

The premise of the story was that it featured a man who had a wife and a mistress, and I played the part of the mistress, except that the character I played could hardly be described as a temptress because all she ever did was to cook him meals as his wife had him on a strict diet.

It ran for three years, spread over three series and 19 episodes. By this point in my life, I seemed to have become pigeon-holed as a comedy actress, and while I considered that I had a great deal more to offer, I was delighted to go along with it because, once again, the scripts were excellent and the programmes were very funny. My co-stars were the late Dinsdale Landon (who was replaced by Terry Brady), Joanna Van Gyseghem and Nichola McAuliffe. Dinsdale, who was a fantastic raconteur, became close friend and remained so until his death.

It was a series that featured a very happy cast. We all got along famously, and we used to rehearse in The Barracks on The King's Road – the beauty of it was that there was ample parking space. I believe it has now been ripped apart and has been replaced with flats. Oh yes, and we could go shopping in The King's Road. Wonderful!

I have always loved reading and am fascinated by books. I cannot get enough of them, and while I was doing *Pig in the Middle* I stumbled across a wonderful shop, John Sandoe Books, and opened an account with them which I still have to this day. It is a proper book shop, staffed by people who not only care about books but who know about them.

I could phone them up and say: "I know this is going to sound daft but there is a book that has been published recently, and I don't know the title, but I am pretty sure it has the word 'Romans' in it somewhere. Can you help me?"

You don't need me to tell you that the average High Street book shop would say no, probably without any hesitation. But not the staff at John Sandoe. They take the time to go through every recent title featuring the word 'Romans' until they come up with the one that rings a bell, and gives you that eureka moment. They are marvellous.

I could also go to them and give them an idea of the plot of a book I had heard about and, again, there will always be somebody who will know what it is called.

I mentioned that two significant events occurred in 1980 – the other was meeting the singer Alvin Stardust. It was in the days when Eamonn Andrews used to host *This is Your Life* and the 'victim' was Michael Aspel. Back in those days, Michael hosted the odd game show, and it was at a time when I seemed to be doing game shows all the time – I did *Child's Play* with him, which was all about the things that children say. And I would go on to work with him later in my career in *Give us a Clue*.

Game shows were fun, easy to do and you got paid for having a good time. I did *Blankety Blank* many times, with Les Dawson, who could make people laugh without opening his mouth, and then with Terry Wogan and that stupid long thin microphone he used to hold – every time that Kenny Everett was on the show he used to grab the mike from Terry and bend it in half.

Michael's *This is Your Life* was filmed not long before Christmas 1980, and Alvin, who was also a guest, chatted me up. I wasn't going out with anybody at the time, I was flattered and, in any event, the pair of us just sort of clicked.

We began dating and within a few months he had moved in with me. I thought: "How on earth did that happen?" We were married the following year. My daughter, Sophie, came along in September 1981 and Alvin and I were married in December 1981. He'd had his name changed by deed poll, but I was officially Mrs Liza Jewry (his original name).

There had been a huge fuss in the press about us living together, having a baby and not being married so I told them: "Well I don't want to get married until I have slimmed down sufficiently to get into a wedding dress." That then caused another furore, and I was accused of being vain, but it was just a flippant, throwaway remark. I may be many things, but vain is not one of them.

More recently, Stephen Fry landed himself in hot water when he said that women didn't really enjoy sex. That was also a flippant remark, but all of a sudden he found himself the subject of all sorts of vicious attacks in the media, and it sparked off a huge debate. Does nobody have a sense of humour anymore?

I don't know why I married Alvin because I genuinely didn't want to get married again, and we didn't have a big wedding. I didn't even tell my mother because I knew she would be cross and would disapprove of what I was doing. In the end, we were happy for a long time.

There was a good deal of media intrusion into our relationship, and some of it was quite hurtful. For instance, the tabloids all wanted to know why this 'English rose' (me) would want to get together with this ageing rocker (Alvin). It was none of their business. We got together because we fell in love. It was as simple as that, and it was nobody's business but ours. The press were trying to portray our relationship as a mismatch – how dare they? And it still goes on today.

In some ways it was actually quite exciting to think that the press were so interested in me, my partner and our relationship, so I was happy to talk to them, but then I realised that my words were being twisted and that they were only reporting the things they wanted to record, and it is sad but true that happy stories don't sell newspapers so they always dig around to see if there is any dirt.

Like most aspiring actresses, I suppose that the thought crossed my mind at some point in my career that I quite fancied trying my hand in America. That was where the big money was to be made, it was where some great television series were being developed and, of course, it was where the film industry was based. Okay, I knew that there was a British film industry but it was small beer when compared with what was happening in Hollywood.

I got my shot at America in the most unexpected way. The Americans loved *Pig in the Middle* and they were looking for a vehicle for Madeline Kahn, who had starred in *Young Frankenstein* with Mel Brooks, but I was told that they also wanted me to appear in the show.

"Now the thing is Liza, we want you to play it as an American. Can you handle that honey?"

Yes, I could handle that, although I should have stood my ground and told them that I was an English actress with an English accent and that if they wanted me then they would have to take me as I was, accent and all. I was always pretty good at doing accents, but the thought did occur to me that if they wanted somebody with an American accent, why didn't they just hire an American actress. But I wasn't going to argue with them, especially when I was told that I was going to be flown out to Los Angeles.

I was sent to a voice coach to work on perfecting my accent and I was quietly becoming rather excited about the prospect of appearing in a prime-time show on US television. I had put my life on hold back in the UK and had signed a provisional five-year contract for the American show – it was telephone numbers and, in all honesty, it was quite scary. This was all done before I had even auditioned for the part, but the contract did not become valid unless I was actually offered the role. While I was going through this process, however, I was not allowed to work for anybody else, so it meant that they couldn't lose. I couldn't get the figures out of my head – we were talking about hundreds of thousands of pounds, and it would have set me and my family up for life. They even spoke to me about where I was going to live and where my children would go to school.

My plan was to bring Alvin and the kids and even my horse over to America to start our new life. Well, that was the plan. The reality turned out to be something rather different. I auditioned for the part – a part I had been playing for three years back home, albeit on this occasion with a phony American accent. And I was stunned to discover that they were going to give the part to somebody else.

So all my dreams came crashing down, and I had to head home. Although I was disappointed, I soon got over it. Yes, the sums of money I would have been bringing in would have changed my life, but did I really want to live and work in the United States?

And in the end it turned out to be a blessing in disguise because Kahn took all the best lines for herself, and the show flopped.

I met a casting director who said he was certain that he could work for me, but I had already made up my mind that America was probably not for me, and I probably didn't believe in myself sufficiently to think that I would be able to get work. Besides, I was an established actress in England, so why would I want to put myself through it all? When I look back on it now I have regrets that I didn't stay on, just to see whether I could have made it in America. It could have been a life-changing experience, but in some respects I suppose it could have been a life-changing experience for all the wrong reasons. Most Hollywood stars lose touch with reality because they earn such vast sums of money and live such cosseted lives, and it could have happened to me. I also wonder if I would have ended up with a face like a wind tunnel, and would my career have lasted? While it is true that image is important in Britain, in the States it is everything and, as a woman, the moment you start to lose your looks you tend to be discarded.

CHAPTER 12
1982 THE GREATEST

"Burton could act the rest of the cast off the screen without even trying, and that is a rare gift. Sadly, demons tend to go hand in hand with genius, and that was certainly true of this wonderful actor."

After I finished filming the second series of *Pig in the Middle*, I was offered a part in *Wagner*. It starred Richard Burton, so it took me about one second to make up my mind that I wanted to do it.

It was a huge production and Burton, of course, took the title role. He was a magnificent actor with this great booming voice and he had an incredible presence. When Burton walked into a room all eyes turned on him, and the talking would stop.

Wagner had an all-star cast, including Laurence Olivier, Joan Plowright, Vanessa Redgrave, John Gielgud, Ralph Richardson, Gemma Craven and Franco Nero. Sometimes you worry before you meet a big movie star, or somebody you admire – you get an image of them in your mind, based on characters they have played. They don't always live up to expectations.

You have to remember that when you see somebody on a screen or on a stage, they are delivering somebody else's lines. In real life, they might actually be quite ordinary. And, indeed, I have met a few stars who have disappointed me. But not Burton. He was an extraordinary man.

I was 32 at the time, but I was still star struck by Burton – it seemed to me that everybody who met him was. People who never met Burton imagine that he was a huge character, and they would be absolutely right. He had charisma, and a personality that sparkled, and it came across on screen. That is what made him such a stupendous actor.

We were sitting in the rain once, waiting to film a scene, when he started reciting poetry. I was mesmerised, and turned to mush. Mind you, had he been reading the phone directory, he would have had the same effect on me. That voice was just fabulous.

He was a friendly, generous and totally accessible at all times. You hear all sorts of stories about the way that stardom turns the heads of some people, and they become impossible to work with, but you could never say that about Burton. When he was younger, he must have had countless beautiful young women falling at his feet, and I could understand why.

We were filming in Hungary and Joan Plowright was playing my mother – another big star, married to Olivier, but again, a delightful woman. I was also in awe of her.

Another time, Burton and Plowright asked me to come and have lunch with them in Burton's trailer. They got talking about the 'old days', and it is one of the biggest regrets of my life that I didn't have a tape recorder with me. I had to pinch myself, just to make sure that I really was sitting having lunch with these two huge stars as they recalled some of the outrageous behaviour that they, and some of the people they had worked with, had indulged in.

When he was at his best, he could act the rest of the cast off the screen without even trying, and that is a rare gift, bestowed on a very small number of people. Sadly, demons tend to go hand in hand with genius, and that was certainly true of this wonderful actor.

All I know is that working alongside him was a privilege, something that I will treasure for the rest of my life.

CHAPTER 13
YOU ARE NICKED

"The biggest difference between Philippa Vale and Robin Hood was that while he gave the proceeds of his deeds of derring-do to the poor, Philippa was interested only in herself."

I consider myself to be incredibly fortunate with some of the parts I have landed. One of the best was when I was cast an upper-class thief called Philippa Vale in the series *Bergerac*, starring John Nettles in the title role. The scripts were among the best I have had the privilege of doing. The writing was fantastic, absolute top drawer.

Jim Bergerac was a detective sergeant working for the Bureau Des Etrangers, with a troubled past – he had an ex-wife on the scene, was a recovering alcoholic and he always seemed to pick the wrong women to fall in love with.

The series ran for 10 years, from 1981 until 1991 and was written by Robert Banks Stewart, creator of another iconic series, *Shoestring*, which starred Trevor Eve. Apart from great scripts, *Bergerac* also boasted a wonderful theme tune, written by George Fenton.

There were some similarities between *Shoestring* and *Bergerac* – Eddie Shoestring returned to work after a nervous breakdown. A Jersey native,

Bergerac returned to the island at the start of the series after recuperating in England following major surgery on his leg following an accident caused by him drinking heavily prior to an attempted arrest. The accident was shown in episode two as a flashback: Bergerac was swigging brandy during a surveillance operation when he noticed his suspect and gave chase. Under the influence of his drinking, he attempted to prevent the man's escape by leaping onto his boat and got his leg crushed against the harbour wall as he slipped back. Upon his return to duty, he was posted to the Bureau des Etrangers.

Fans of the series will know that he drove an old burgundy Triumph Roadster, a car that was not suited to the winding roads of Jersey and its 40mph speed limit. Two different cars were used throughout the series. John Nettles hated the first one because it was very unreliable and also had dreadful brakes, which meant that it was notoriously difficult to stop. It also had a very noisy engine, so the crew used to superimpose a separate soundtrack.

Bergerac dealt with some pretty meaty issues, including one episode where an old man was unmasked as having been a Nazi war criminal.

It was set on the island of Jersey – as you can imagine, it was no hardship to stay there while I was filming my part.

Philippa Vale featured in a number of episodes, the first of which was screened in 1983. Right from the start, Bergerac sensed that there was something dodgy about her, but that didn't stop him becoming smitten with her. For her part, Philippa saw herself as some kind of modern-day Robin Hood. She would only steal jewels from people who could afford to lose them.

The biggest difference between her and Robin Hood, however, was that while he gave the proceeds of his deeds of derring-do to the poor,

99

Philippa was interested only in herself.

I remember one scene where I was required to strip off and run into the sea naked. I had made it clear to the director from a pretty early stage that I was not prepared to do this, so they hired a former page three girl as my body double, and it was her that viewers saw diving into the waves. When I saw the finished episode I have to tell you that I was pretty pleased with it – and I was perfectly happy for everybody to think that the woman with the impossibly perfect body was me.

Inevitably, Philippa seduced Jim Bergerac and had her evil way with him. She was attracted to him, but she also believed that if she could get the detective to fall in love with her then he would never arrest her. Needless to say, Bergerac always played it by the book, and when the time came, he did arrest her and charge her with theft. I lasted until series seven, so I had a pretty good run.

John Nettles is one of the most delightful men that I have ever met – we would be reunited briefly during the series *Midsomer Murders*. There are some actors with whom you discover there is an instant chemistry, and that certainly existed with John and I. It helped to make our characters and the relationship they developed all the more believable. But that was all it ever was – an on-screen relationship. Two actors doing their jobs.

Yes, we became friends off screen, but nothing more than that. He was, and is, a genuinely nice man, somebody that I still count among my friends. When he filmed his last episode of *Midsomer Murders* in 2010, I was asked to the party they held to mark the event, and it was great to catch up with him. Once again, it was a part that he made his own.

People always joke about the body count, and say that they would never want to live in a village where so many of the inhabitants get bumped off, but it is a police drama, and you need to give the officer in charge some crimes to solve. In any event, I believe that the picture-postcard location where the series is shot is almost as much of a star as are the cast.

Anyway, going back to Bergerac and my relationship with John, I was horrified when I picked up *The News of the World* one day and read that I was having an affair with him. It was untrue. As I have said, I adored him, and I know there was a chemistry between us while we were on screen, but he was a friend and nothing went on between us. John wasn't married at the time and I was going through a divorce so it wouldn't have hurt anybody if we had been having a relationship, but we were not.

The tabloids in this country get away with murder and I knew that had I done nothing, the story would have gone away and people would have quickly forgotten about it, but I made up my mind that I wasn't going to let them get away with it. I decided that I was going to make a stand – this was the sort of story that could have destroyed lesser people.

And I was conscious of the fact that it is only natural for people to think that there is no smoke without fire. I was flattered that our on-screen relationship had been so successful that a journalist could be convinced that there must be something going on behind the scenes, but I was also livid that such lies could be written about John and I, so I decided to sue for libel. My solicitor told me not to go ahead with the action unless I was telling the truth because he knew that the paper would do whatever it could to discredit me. But I had truth on my side, and I won.

Of course, at the end of it all I felt completely vindicated, but I thought it was outrageous that nobody had thought to check the facts before printing the story. I still don't know who it was that tipped off the journalist, but my conscience was clear back then and it still is today.

There was a particularly chilling postscript to the series. In Bergerac, the bureau was located at Haut de la Garenne, a former children's home which in February 2008 became the focus of the Jersey child abuse investigation in 2008. The building ceased being a children's home in 1983 and was re-opened as Jersey's first and only youth hostel.

There have been several actors with whom I have had a chemistry, people who you just know you will work well with. It is nothing new – look at Spencer Tracey and Katharine Hepburn, Richard Burton and Elizabeth Taylor. I know that these were people who also had relationships off screen, but there was an electricity between them when the cameras started to roll.

When people are on your wavelength it is easy to work with them, so you want to work with them all the time, and that is why Alan Ayckbourn likes to use people he has worked with before. There are a few Ayckbourn actors I have been fortunate enough to have worked with, such as Adrian McLoughlin, Terence Booth, Matthew Cottle, Alexandra Mathie, Laura Dodington. They all know how to do Alan's plays and are wonderful people to work with, even though none of them are household names. They get what Alan's plays are all about and are fantastic on stage. The set could fall down and you could forget all your lines, but they would carry on, totally unfazed by it all. That is a gift few people have.

I work with them and I know that I am in safe hands. Anything could happen.

Speaking of distractions, I once appeared in a play during which there was a commotion in the audience during the performance. You are taught from a very early age that you should carry on with the show, no matter what is going on, and that is precisely what we did, only to be told at the end that a member of the audience had suffered a heart attack and died. I do hope it had nothing to do with my performance!

CHAPTER 14
1983 IS THERE A DOCTOR
IN THE HOUSE?

"Dominic Guard and I played a pair of highly incompetent space raiders, so inept that every time we drew our guns, the ends fell off."

There are several cult TV series in Britain, and chief among them must be *Dr Who*. Yes it has gone through all sorts of changes, and at one point during its life it seemed that the entire special effects budget stretched to about £1.50. But children always loved it, and everybody, but everybody has their own favourite Doctor.

For some it might be Jon Pertwee, for others William Hartnell. There will be votes for Colin Baker and his namesake Tom and, of course, a huge groundswell of public opinion in favour of David Tennent, who was so instrumental in ensuring the success of its relaunch.

My own personal favourite is none of the above. Instead, it is the incomparable Peter Davison, who made his name playing the loveable Tristan Farnham in *All Creatures Great and Small*.

Why would I pick Peter? That's easy. He was the one I starred with when I appeared in the series. I didn't know it at the time, but *Dr Who* would follow me for the rest of my life, and in some of the oddest places.

Peter is a genuinely lovely man, somebody I worked with on a couple of other projects, including *Tales of the Unexpected* for Anglia TV, and I think that he was a wonderful Doctor. This was a particularly hectic period in my life, when I was juggling being a wife and mother, and I was making the third and final series of *Pig in the Middle*, and doing various one-off appearances in other shows.

We filmed four episodes and Dominic Guard and I played a pair of highly incompetent space raiders, so inept that every time we drew our guns, the ends fell off. And there was a marvellous monster in it played by a man called R J Bell. He had to spend hours on end inside a rubber suit – you can imagine how hot it was inside that costume, so it was no surprise that he regularly used to pass out. The crew would then remove him, take off the monster's head and get him out in the fresh air until such time as he had recovered.

The storyline was not too dissimilar to *Alien*, the classic space movie starring Sigourney Weaver, although it was written and filmed long before the movie. Basically, there had been a plague that had claimed the lives of lots of people and it was the Doctor's job to save the world. Nothing new there really. We also had lots of people made up as lepers. It was hilarious in the BBC canteen at lunchtime because none of us had time to get changed, so you would have Peter sitting at a table having his lunch with a leper on one side and a monster on the other. And nobody ever batted an eyelid.

My outstanding memory of it all was that it was an incredibly happy time in my life. Everybody took the work seriously enough, but we laughed a lot too. In fact, I have been lucky enough to have experienced that sort of sensation throughout my career, working with creative people who like to have fun. It has been an absolute joy.

It was officially classed as a children's series but it crossed over and appealed just as much to adults as it did to their offspring. I grew up with William Hartnell and then Patrick Troughton as Dr Who – those were the days when it was filmed in black and white, and I always thought it was quite dark and scary. Then there were the Daleks – we were all terrified of them, without realising that they couldn't even climb a flight of stairs!

In many ways, appearing in *Dr Who* changed my life forever because I came to realise that I had appeared in a series that had a truly worldwide following and meant a great deal to the people who watched it – they have fan club meetings in America, for goodness sake. Even now, the old Doctors and series regulars do very nicely out of the programme thank you very much, and are regularly flown out to places such as America to attend various conventions. It is quite astonishing.

My only Dr Who convention took place in a pub in Chiswick. I had been appearing in panto in Norwich and discovered that one of the back-stage crew was the secretary of the *Dr Who* fan club. We got talking and she asked me if I would like to attend a meeting. Well of course I said yes.

And so it was that I ended up talking to a group of hard-core *Dr Who* fans. The most difficult part was at the end when I had to sign autographs – they arrived with all sorts of photos of when I was in the programme and, of course, they wanted me to sign them all.

CHAPTER 15
LIZA GODDARD,
THIS IS YOUR LIFE

"People had been behaving rather oddly. Susan Jameson took me to a race meeting at Cheltenham on a bitterly cold winter's day. People were coming out of the woodwork and asking me out."

In 1983 I was part of something called The Theatre of Comedy, set up by playwright Ray Cooney, together with a group of fellow actors (including Judi Dench, Richard Briers, Leslie Phillips, Michael Williams, John Alderton, Pauline Collins, Bill Pertwee, Tom Conti and Geoffrey Palmer), directors and writers. We took out a lease on the Shaftesbury Theatre, and the aim was to present the best of British comedy writing, both at the Shaftesbury and other West End theatres. Its early seasons were a huge success, allowing the company to purchase the freehold of the theatre in 1984. The current chairman, Don Taffner OBE, joined the company in 1986 and became the majority shareholder in control of the management of the company in 1992.

The company's success extended beyond the Shaftesbury Theatre, producing and co-producing a number of notable regional and West End productions, including Alan Ayckbourn's *Intimate Exchanges*; Peter

Nichols' *Passion Play* with Leslie Phillips; *Hay Fever* at the Albery Theatre and the successful revival of *The Prime of Miss Jean Brodie* starring Patricia Hodge. The company received many accolades, including two Olivier Awards in 1986, and is still going strong today. I was thrilled to be a part of it and served on several committees and suchlike.

See How They Run was the very first show. Ray rewrote it, and by the time he had finished it was an extraordinary piece of work, and I was delighted to be asked to appear in it alongside Christopher Timothy, who played my husband, and Royce Mills, who is one of the funniest people I have ever worked with. I appeared with him in pantomime and he plays a wonderful dame. Michael Denison also appeared in *See How They Run* – he was and is the perfect English gentleman.

I appeared with Dinsdale Landon in *Wife Begins at Forty* at the Vaudeville theatre in London. Once again, it wasn't terribly good, but it had a marvellous 20 minutes or so at the end, so Ray took it away and did a lot of work on it, and phoned me and said: "Liza, if I write a part for your dog, will you do this play?"

"Of course I will Ray."

Gertrude, my golden retriever, had already appeared in *See How They Run*, and was brilliant. She loved being on stage and revelled in all the attention she got, a natural performer. Gertrude and I had a rare old time, spending ten months in the West End, and she obviously shared a dressing room with me. She was such an extraordinarily gifted dog that, after a while, she knew her cue and ended up stealing the show every night.

During the run, I had to take a few days off because I had been struck down with flu – they had an understudy for me, but not for Gertrude, so while I lay in bed recovering, the theatre sent a taxi for Gertrude and she happily clambered in and got out when the cab arrived at the theatre. She did it perfectly well without me, and then came home in a taxi when the play was over.

She also loved going out for dinner. We used to eat regularly at The Ivy, where she was made very welcome, and there was a new Italian restaurant that she absolutely loved because it had marble flooring and she adored lying on it because it kept her cool. I got Gertrude from James Bolam and Susan Jameson after their dog, Rosie, had puppies. Animals have played a huge part in my life, and it is a subject that I will return to later.

When we did *Wife Begins at Forty*, the place was packed solid every night. Or at least it was, right up until the moment that Ronald Reagan decided to bomb Libya and London emptied.

Having appeared as a guest on *This is Your Life*, I never for one moment considered that I would ever be caught out, but I was. It happened in 1983. I'd had a phone call from Ray Cooney, inviting me to a do that was supposedly connected to The Theatre of Comedy. He insisted that I had to dress up nicely – not that I wouldn't have anyway.

People had been behaving rather oddly. Susan Jameson, one of my co-stars in *Take Three Girls*, and somebody with whom I established a lifelong friendship, took me to a race meeting at Cheltenham on a bitterly cold winter's day. Suddenly, people were coming out of the woodwork and asking me out, and of course it was because the producers wanted to make sure I was out of the way while they spoke to my family and rifled through old family photograph albums.

We were on stage at the Shaftesbury Theatre or an alleged charity do when Eamonn suddenly appeared on stage, carrying the big red book, and I thought: "Oh my God, it's somebody's *This is Your Life*." I looked around and there was Paul Eddington, Michael Denison, Tom Conti, Pauline Collins and Maureen Lipman and I wondered which one of them it was going to be. I took a step backwards to move out of the limelight, but Eamonn homed in on me and uttered those unforgettable words, "Liza Goddard, This is your life..." I could not believe it was me – it was a huge shock.

When I got over the initial shock and was being taken to the studio in Holborn where the show was to be filmed my biggest worry was whether or not I would know everybody. For those of you who are not old enough to remember the programme, there would be a voice relating some experience from the life of the central character – would I remember them all, or would I end up making a fool of myself?

The next thought that entered my mind was: "What are they going to say about me?" I suppose the good thing was that everybody who appeared did so because they wanted to and because they were on my side, so any worries I might have had turned out to be groundless. The guests included Christopher Biggins and the entire cast of The Theatre of Comedy. There was Richard Briers, Derek Nimmo, Bill Pertwee, Donald Sinden, Leslie Phillips, Frank Finlay, Carol Hawkins (who starred in *Please Sir* and *Bless this House*) – a very illustrious group of people.

The producers also managed to track down some of my old school friends, and it was quite something to be reunited with them all and to find out what they had all done with their lives. And then there was a satellite link with Australia featuring Googie Withers and John McCallum, who were there to speak about *Skippy*. They even flew over Garry Pankhurst, who had played Sonny in the series – that was quite an achievement because he didn't really pursue his acting career after

Skippy and was actually was a shy man.

Charlotte Bingham and Terry Brady, who wrote so much of the comedy in which I made my name, came on and said some very kind things about me, as did Susan Jameson and Angela Down, my co-stars from *Take Three Girls*.

They always liked to wheel out well-known people, so Russell Grant, with whom I was great friends at the time, appeared, and the biggest surprise of all was Maureen O'Hara, who was Mia Farrow's mother. I had worked with her in *No Sex Please*, and she agreed to do a satellite link from America. She was a wonderfully dotty lady. I mentioned earlier that one of the great influences upon my life had been Miss Eggar, my teacher, and they tracked her down too.

Best of all, nobody said anything that embarrassed me. I had been worried that somebody might come up with a story that would make me cringe, but it didn't happen. Mind you, nobody would ever rubbish you on a programme such as This Is Your Life, although I felt that everybody was totally genuine with their comments, and it made me feel very special.

Of course, my Mum and Dad were there – they had been divorced for some time by that point, so it was quite something to get them on the same programme together as they had split on far from good terms and didn't talk to each other.

Thom, who was eight years old at the time, came out clutching a teddy bear that he still has to this day. Alvin was wearing an extraordinary leather top, which was very 1980s. I was wearing a Bruce Oldfield frock which featured lots of sequins and I wish that I still had it because not only was it fabulous, but it is a style that is back in fashion.

They flew my sister over from America for the show, and at the end they brought Sophie out on a Shetland pony, led out by a man called Phil Gardner (Phil was a very special person in my life and I will tell you more about him later) – that was a tremendous moment. The party they put on afterwards was amazing too.

I had often wondered about the big red book. During the programme, it was Eamonn's script and although he handed it over to me at the end, it was taken away, and I later received another copy, this time filled with fabulous photographs. It was, and remains, a great keepsake.

Around the same time, Dave Lee Travis, or the Hairy Monster as he liked to call himself, was compiling a book in which he asked various celebrities what they liked and disliked about themselves and I contributed by saying that I was quite happy with my face and my feet, but I wasn't terribly happy with the rest of my body, so I had a photograph taken for the book in which every other part of my body was covered up. It was quite bizarre. And I can't understand why I felt the way I did because, especially when you are young, you should celebrate your body and give thanks for your health, rather than peering in a mirror and trying to find fault with yourself.

At this point, I should also mention Barry Burnett, who was my agent for around 20 years, and I was incredibly lucky to have him. Some agents just sit back and wait for the work to come in and then count their commission. Not Barry. He was a grafter who strived to do the best for all his clients.

Agents are important. When I was at the height of my career, you might well imagine that the parts simply came along and the contracts were stuck under my nose to be signed, but that is to over-simplify matters. Barry would go through my contracts with a fine-toothed comb and he would not let me see it until he felt that the money I was being offered was right. It was also his job to sort out the wheat from the chafe because at that time I was being offered a lot of work. Some of it was superb, but a lot of it was work that I wouldn't have touched with a barge-pole. The great thing about Barry was that he had a feel for the roles that would work for me and the ones that would not. If he felt a part was either rubbish or that the money on offer wasn't enough, he wouldn't even trouble me with it. He was very good at doing the deal for me.

I am fortunate enough to be able to say that there isn't a single part I turned down and later thought: "Why did I do that?" Like every other actress in the business, I have missed out on parts that I wanted, but in many cases it has been because I was committed to a theatre run and there simply hasn't been the time or the opportunity to wait for me to become free. There was a part in *The Royal*, for instance, that I missed out on because I was appearing in a play, and *The Royal* went on to become a highly successful series.

It's a funny thing, but I was in a shop recently browsing through CDs and DVDs and it occurred to me that lots of old TV shows are now available once again – except for the stuff I have been in. The BBC had this habit of taping over things for many years, and ITV, for whom I did many of my comedy series, didn't keep things either.

Roll Over Beethoven, which I made in the early 1980s, is the perfect example of a series that would have made a perfect boxed set. It was about a rock star (Nigel Planer) who moved to the country and couldn't actually play the piano so he ended up going for lessons. I played a very uptight middle-class piano teacher, and the thread of the story was the middle-class clashing with the working class, and resenting this pop star who had become extremely rich without being able to play the piano. It was written by Laurence Marks and Maurice Gran, who went on to write *Birds of a Feather*. Just to emphasise the quality of the team, the script producers were Dick Clement and Ian La Franais, who wrote *The Likely Lads*, *Porridge*, *Lovejoy* and *Auf Wiedersehen, Pet*.

One day we did a run-through and at the end of it all we knew that it wasn't quite working – there was a missing ingredient. Ian La Frenais suddenly clicked his fingers and said: "I've got it. I think it will work if we do this..." and he grabbed a piece of paper and couldn't write down his ideas fast enough. It was a privilege to see a master of his craft in action like that. It goes without saying that by the time he had finished everything was perfect.

It was one of the first television comedies to be filmed without a studio audience, which was almost unheard of in those days and I was excited to be in at the start of that. Nigel was brilliant in that show. Sadly, it appears to have been lost forever. It also featured one of the earliest appearances of Neil Morrissey, who later went on to find fame and fortune in *Men Behaving Badly*. Neil played a member of the band, and it was obvious that he had a comic talent.

Throughout my career I have worked with many fine young actors and actresses whom I have known possess the talent to become real stars, but so much of it is down to luck in my profession, being in the right place at the right time when the right director or agent happens to be around.

Luck plays a huge part. If you look at my career as an example. *Skippy* was never planned. I just happened to wander into an audition and, fortunately, found a director who saw a talent in me, or who at least saw in me the Clancy that he had imagined from reading the scripts. If I hadn't got that part and made enough money to make my trip back to

London then I may well have remained in Australia and might never have been offered another TV role.

And then when I got to London and was sent up to audition for *Take Three Girls*, what would have happened had I not got that part? But I did, and it helped to set me up for a decent career in Britain. Right place, right time.

When you look at films and somebody wins an Oscar, it is amazing how often that actor or actress has been fifth or sixth choice because others have either turned it down or have had other commitments. I often wonder how the people who turned it down originally feel when they go along to the awards ceremony and see somebody else called on stage to pick up the statuette. It should always be remembered though that just because one person wins an Oscar for a movie role, it doesn't necessarily mean that somebody else doing the same part would have won it.

CHAPTER 16
ALL CLUED UP

One of the joys of my life was the time I spent doing *Give us a Clue*. It ran from 1979 until 1992 and was hosted by Michael Aspel (1979 until 1983) and Michael Parkinson (1984 until 1992). In case you missed it, it was based on charades, a party game where players used mime rather than speaking to demonstrate a name, phrase, book, play, film or TV programme. Each player was given roughly two minutes to act out their given subject in front of his/her team, and if the others were unsuccessful in guessing correctly, the opposing team would have a chance to answer for a bonus point.

Originally, one team was captained by Lionel Blair and the other by Una Stubbs.

I first appeared on the show as a guest in 1979 and appeared many times after that when Una was the captain. I loved the show and we got paid for doing it, but it wasn't like work at all. When Una left, Lionel told the producers that he thought I was a natural to take her place and, lo and behold, they offered it me and I was thrilled to bits to accept.

I ended up doing 150 episodes. We used to film five a day over a 17-day stretch. You may wonder how it was possible to remain fresh and enthusiastic with such a schedule but it wasn't a problem because we had so much fun making the programmes. And when you are around a man like Lionel, it is impossible to become stale. I used to be shattered at the end of each day, but not him. He was and is a remarkable man, who lives to perform.

The way it worked was that all the guests would turn up for lunch and we would all sit down, have something to eat and have a chat about the shows, then we would film two in the afternoon. We would then stop for something else to eat and the people who had done the afternoon shows would often stay with us while the new teams arrived for the evening shows. Every day it was like having a showbiz party, with people cracking jokes and telling stories.

After we had eaten, we would film three more shows in the evening, always in front of an audience. We would finish the day with a drink at the bar and then everybody would head home.

Lionel used to take it all quite seriously and he would get furious with his team if they couldn't work out his clues – it was hilarious. We used to have people such as Jimmy Tarbuck on regularly and of course the thing with comedians is that they will always go for the gags rather than playing the game, and I swear that there were times when you could see the steam coming out of Lionel's ears.

Poor old Parky would end up weeping with laughter at the combined antics of the comedians and Lionel. There were no prizes at stake, just pride, and the only reason that the show came to an end was because Thames Television, who produced it, lost their franchise.

Because we did so many shows, it meant that I had to have dozens of changes of clothing. I love clothes, so trust me when I tell you that it was no hardship to go around borrowing different outfits from shops in The Strand. Remember that if we did five shows in a day it meant that I had to have five changes of costume. One of the perks of my profession is that you get to wear some fabulous clothes and sometimes there were outfits that I loved so much that I just had to have them. I should point out that we were never given them – if you want something, you have to pay for it. And because the costumes have to last, they were almost always top quality.

One of my other abiding memories of the programme is that Lionel and I seemed to always end up equal – it seemed that nobody ever won. I also got to work with some of my best friends in the business, people like Susan Jameson and Linda Bellingham, who were and are women who enjoy having a good laugh, and also liked to play the game. On one occasion I had Hinge and Brackett on my team and we won, but Lionel said that we had cheated.

"Cheated? What do you mean?"

"Because they are men."

"You are saying that men are better than women are you Lionel?"

"You cheated."

When you watched each episode on television it lasted for half an hour, but I can assure you that it took an awful lot longer than that to film each one. If we were lucky, and had a following wind at our backs, then we could do it in around an hour. By the end of the series they were giving us song titles with 24 words – can you imagine how difficult it was to mime that?

It was good clean family fun, and I am convinced it would do really well if it was to be revived today.

Like many other women in the late 1970s and early '80s, I decided to have my hair permed. Why did nobody tell me? Who did nobody take me to one side and tell me that, years later, I would sit down and look at pictures of myself taken during that time and shudder.

I thank the Lord for one thing though – at least I wasn't alone. All over the land there are women who have looked through photograph albums in recent years and wondered what on earth it was that caused them to take leave of their senses and part with huge amounts of money to have their hair turned to frizz. And it wasn't just women – hands up everybody who remembers Kevin Keegan?

Mine was at its worst when I was doing *Give us a Clue*, and what makes it worse is that now, all these years later, clips of that series are still shown on a fairly regular basis. I remember that I always wanted curly hair, but the funny thing is that people who have curly hair spend their lives wishing that it was straight. It's the old thing about wanting what you can't have.

CHAPTER 17
GROWING APART

"I was away from home for long periods and, inevitably, you start to drift apart and become total strangers to one another."

After my Hollywood disappointment with *Pig in the Middle*, I came home to my husband and my two children. I bought a horse, a Hanoverian called Olive, and we moved to a village called Dunsfold in the Surrey countryside. One of the reasons for our move was to be close to Sue Jameson and James Bolam, who are lifelong friends with whom I have shared many, many wonderful times.

Alvin and I were married for eight years, but if I am honest, it was a bit like my marriage to Colin Baker – I leapt in too quickly, and got married to him too soon. Once again, we should just have remained friends.

Leaping in without thinking about the consequences is just about the story of my life, but I will always be thankful to Alvin for Sophie. And we did remain friends.

It also didn't help that I was working really hard. We lived in Surrey and I spent a great deal of time working in the West End, including 10 months in Ray Cooney's *Wife Begins at Forty*. I was also doing a lot of TV work during the day – this all goes back to my fear about the work suddenly drying up and the calls stopping, so I grabbed just about everything I was offered back then, but it was no way to keep a loving relationship going, and I suppose I knew that at the time. I was still making *Pig in the Middle* and then there was *Bergerac* and *Dr Who*.

It meant I was away from home for long periods and, inevitably, you start to drift apart and become total strangers to one another. He wasn't doing a huge amount of work, and it all put a tremendous strain on our marriage. And when he did get work, of course he took it, so that meant I might be home and he was away. Living in Surrey was great, but running backwards and forwards to London was hard work and it took its toll on me – I was permanently exhausted and, as such, I suppose that you become a bit tetchy. It would have been easier to have not had a horse and to have lived in London, thus slashing the commuting time, but I didn't see it that way.

I tried to convince myself that I was doing it for the children, to give them the country life, and that would have been fine if I had been able to enjoy it with them, but there never seemed to be enough money, so I had to keep working, and the more I worked the less I saw of them and the more tired I felt. I felt as if I was on a treadmill and although the solution was in my own hands, I refused to accept it. I suppose what I needed was somebody to sit me down and make me face up to things.

To the outsider, and I suppose even to some of our friends and family, we appeared to be living a fantasy lifestyle, when nothing could have been further from the truth. On the occasions when Alvin and I were together, I never seemed to have the energy to do anything with him – I just wanted to blank everything out, put my feet up and relax, or go out and ride Olive.

I chose to do all my travel by car, and there were times when I got behind the wheel and struggled to keep my eyes open. I was really lucky that I didn't have a serious accident, or cause one. I would frequently get in the car and arrive at my destination and sit bolt upright and wonder how I had got there because I would have been thinking about so many other things, and would drive the car on auto-pilot. And then it seemed to me that the moment I walked through the front door, I was expected to take over everything, whether that be looking after the children, cooking dinner, tidying up or whatever.

Because I was working so much, I was spending all my time with other people, and when I did sit down with Alvin there didn't seem to be much to say to one another and we no longer seemed to even share interests in common. .

During this time, I was filming *Bergerac*, and that meant spending two weeks in Jersey. Increasingly, I found myself looking forward to those weeks because it meant that I was in a place that I loved, working with a fantastic cast and crew, and I didn't have to get in a car at the end of each day and drive home and pretend to be a domestic goddess. Making *Bergerac* was work, of course it was, but to me it was more like a holiday, and I suppose that when you start to look forward to being away from home, that is when you know there is something not quite right with your life.

Then it would be over and I would find myself back home again working like a slave and asking myself: "Why am I doing this?" Please don't get the wrong idea about Alvin – I am not suggesting for one moment that he didn't pull his weight around the house. He was away for much of the time as well. No, the problem was the lifestyle that I had chosen for us, but I refused to admit it.

Life became very fragmented, and there was also the question of arranging child care and employing a nanny or an au pair. We had some wonderful Spanish au pairs but in some respects it was almost like having another child in the house, except that I had to pay for this one. Mother also used to help out from time to time.

Probably the worst experience of my entire life happened when I was married to Alvin. Sophie was three months old and we had employed a nanny to help us out. As an actress you don't get maternity pay, so if you are not working then you are not earning. It meant that I had to go back to work as soon as possible.

It was before we moved to the country. We were living in Muswell Hill and the nanny slipped and dropped Sophie down the stairs. The poor child hit her head on the floor and fractured her skull in four places. We rushed her to the Whittington hospital and we certainly didn't need a doctor to tell us that it was serious. We just knew she had been badly injured. It was an absolutely hideous ordeal.

I remember sitting in the waiting room, expecting a doctor to come out and tell me that my beautiful baby girl was dead. I looked round the children's ward, and it was filthy. It was the middle of winter and there was a hole in one of the windows – it was like something out of Dickens.

To make matters worse, the press gathered outside the hospital and began speculating that Alvin had thrown Sophie down the stairs in some kind of fit of rage. He wasn't even in the house when it happened. It was absolutely ludicrous. Ironically, there had been a photographer in the house at the time of the accident because we were doing a piece for a magazine, and he was getting ready to take a picture of me with Sophie when the nanny slipped.

And it didn't end there – the next thing we knew was that social

123

services were at our house wanting to speak to Alvin to find out if he had played any part in what had happened. They said they needed to be sure that he wasn't violent. I know that they were only doing their jobs, and I also know that there are some people who do mistreat babies, but what made my blood boil about this was the fact that it had been the press who had come up with idea that my husband, the father of this child, had been responsible. There had never been anything to suggest that Alvin had a temper. And if he had thrown Sophie down the stairs, don't you think that I would have been the first person to tell the authorities what he had done?

As if we didn't have enough to worry about at the time. It was an accident, pure and simple. Our nanny was wearing socks on carpeted stairs and lost her footing. Fact! It was stupidity, but it was not wilful.

The hospital Sophie was admitted to had been designed by Florence Nightingale, and it was in a shocking state. I was so appalled at the state of the ward in which Sophie was being cared for that I went out and bought rubber gloves and Dettol and cleaned her area of it from top to bottom. I later discovered that the cleaner was off with flu, and there was nobody to replace her. Remember that we are talking about a hospital here. It was filthy.

To make matters worse, there was a broken window, and the snow used to come in through it.

I sat with her for days, quietly praying. Because she was only three months old, there was a limit to what the doctors could do, so we just had to watch, wait and monitor her progress and hope for the best. Eventually she recovered and we were told that she could go home. I was warned that she might have problems when she reached puberty, that there was every chance that she might suffer from epilepsy, but puberty came and went without incident, albeit that it was a very worrying time and I seemed to spend months watching her every move, just in case. I am thrilled to say that she grew into a healthy young woman.

As for the nanny, I wanted to fire her on the spot, but Alvin took a different view, pointing out that she hadn't done it on purpose, that it had been an accident and that we should keep her on. And we did. Needless to say, she was almost as devastated by what had happened as we were. She stayed on for a while, but eventually left.

Returning to the subject of the media, apart from those couple of painful experiences during my time with Alvin, I have to say that throughout my career I have mostly had a pretty good relationship with them. I suppose that fame was treated differently back in those days though, and journalists were not as intrusive as they are now. I feel sorry for today's celebrities because it seems to me that they can't breathe without it being photographed and appearing in one magazine or another. Of course it is also true that some of them can't get enough of the press.

In those days I could go out for a meal with Alvin, who was a star in his own right remember, and people would usually leave us alone. There might be the odd one who would ask for an autograph or say that they had liked a show I had been in, but we were not seen as public property. We never had to put bars on windows or install security cameras, as we were allowed get on with leading normal lives.

I regard myself as being pretty lucky to have been able to live what I would regard as a low-profile life, and the public have been happy to let me live it.

And the fact that I have been married three times has nothing to do with my profile as an actress. It has simply been down to me making two bad choices. As far as Alvin was concerned I suppose the final nail in our coffin was when he discovered God – on a train to Waterloo. He was converted by a group of people he had shared a carriage with – the cleaners got on board and found them all kneeling on the floor praying to God. He came home that day and announced: "I've found God." Right you are then!

I would never knock anybody for their beliefs, and I accept that God moves in mysterious ways and affects different people in different ways, but this wasn't for me. I found it all pretty trying, although I did go along with him to a few meetings. I believe that people who go through this sort of experience do so because they have been searching for something, and good luck to those who find it. It turned out to be good for him – he became a Baptist, and he still is to this day.

When we put everything together, we both realised that we wanted different things out of life. His religious conversion was by no means the only reason we finally split up. As when any relationship ends, there were a whole host of contributory factors.

So that led to divorce number two, something I would never wish upon anybody. It is a beastly experience in which there are never any winners. You have to divide everything up and then I had to move to a smaller house, back in Farnham. It was all terribly painful and a low time in my life, although I did also feel a certain sense of relief that it had come to an end.

Like Colin, Alvin remarried (to a woman called Julie) and found the ideal partner because, like him, she was also a Baptist. They had a daughter and remain blissfully happy.

Alvin still tours, wearing platform boots and a wig, and he still plays an important part in Sophie's life. The thing about rock'n'rollers such as Alvin is that they are fantastic performers and when you go to see them play you know that you are going to be entertained. When Sophie turned 21 we put on a party for her, with a local band playing. It was a good night, and the music was okay, but it was only when Alvin got up on stage and started to sing that the party really got going. He was brilliant, and got everybody up on the floor dancing. He had been a chorister as a boy so he possessed a 'proper' voice, and still does.

When Alvin was at the height of his career, he had to pay for everything himself, and only if there was anything left could he call that his own. The manager would take 20-25%, and then Alvin and his band would fork out for transport, hotels, backing singers – the lot. It is hardly surprising that so many acts ended up with nothing despite perhaps having had a string of chart hits. The problem was that they were so desperate to get a record deal and follow their dream that they would have signed just about anything without reading it first. It was the promoters and the managers who made all the money.

Through him I got to meet Paul McCartney. What a thrill that was. Alvin's first wife, Iris, had a brother who was Rory Storm of Rory Storm and the Hurricanes fame, and their drummer was a certain Ringo Starr. So Alvin mixed with a lot of very famous people right from the start of his career. I believe that Iris may even have been one of Paul McCartney's very first girlfriends.

All the musicians from that era are still amazing – McCartney, The Rolling Stones, The Who. And it is because they were proper musicians, not manufactured like so many of today's groups and solo artists. Not so long ago I went to see James Taylor, the American singer-songwriter, and he still has a fantastic voice. I was spellbound by his performance.

In 1987, at around the time Alvin and I split up, Ray Cooney asked me if I would tour *Wife Begins at Forty* in Australia. I needed to get away from England and felt that a change of scenery would work wonders, even though I do admit that going all the way to Australia may seem somewhat extreme. Just before we were due to leave, the south of England was struck by the worst hurricane in living memory – it was so bad that I wasn't able to get out of my house because of all the trees that had been blown down.

The local men announced that they would round up everybody who owned a chain saw and would soon have all the debris out of the way, and things back to normal. That was fine, apart from the fact that everybody owned electric chain saws, and there was no electricity, so the men all ended up taking refuge in the local pub.

Eventually, we got the roads open but we had no power for ten days, and that meant we also had no hot water. Fortunately, the nearby farm had a Rayburn, which heated their water, and the cowman's wife, Goody, more or less threw open her front door for anybody who wanted to come along and have a bath.

Despite all of that, we got to Australia, starting off in Adelaide, and also playing in Perth and Melbourne. Dear old Jimmy Edwards, who had fled to Australia after being outed as a gay, was in the cast, and was still understandably bitter about the way he had been treated by the media back in England. It was all so incredibly unfair. Nowadays, nobody would bat an eyelid.

I thoroughly enjoyed my time back in Australia, not least because my mother flew out with Sophie. While we were there, the country celebrated its bicentenary and we went to Sydney for that – what a party the Aussies put on.

I started off appearing opposite Hywel Bennett, who suffered a minor nervous breakdown and had to be flown home from Adelaide. Ray Cooney had to abandon a holiday in Hawaii, fly out to Australia and take over the part from Bennett.

After 18 weeks Down Under, I flew back to England and sold the house in Surrey then moved back to Farnham to be close to my mother. I bought a picture-postcard cottage at the end of a dirt track in a place called Bourne. The doorway into the bedroom had an iron bar running across the top and I lost count of the number of times I nearly knocked myself out on it.

By this point in my life I had two children, no husband, a horse and about nine dogs. I have always had a soft spot for animals, and people kept giving me their dogs. The house became like an RSPCA rescue centre.

One of the great joys was that I could get on my horse and ride for miles in unspoilt countryside. It was idyllic and I loved it. One of my favourite rides was across an area known as Hankley Common and I would often take the dogs with me. There was one occasion when I was out for a ride and I had my golden retriever with me. As we crossed the common I looked down and saw a young soldier in a foxhole.

"Good morning."

"Good morning ma'am."

The Army were out on manoeuvres. A little further along there was another soldier, then there was a tent, and then there was a much bigger tent. I realised my dog had disappeared and suddenly I heard somebody swearing.

"Bloody dog..." She had followed the scent of the food and was running amok in the mess. Needless to say, we were not terribly popular.

I told the soldiers I had never seen the dog before in my life, but I don't think they believed me.

I had a wonderful lurcher called Clark, as in Clark Kent. I had done some charity work for the Canine Defence League with Jilly Cooper and she was smitten by the dog.

"Liza I would love to take it home, but I just can't."

"Don't worry then. I will have him."

It seemed that wherever I went, I acquired another dog and, of course, it created a unique set of problems when I had to go away to work. You cannot put dogs into kennels for weeks on end – quite apart from anything else, it would have cost me a not-so-small fortune. So I had to find some reliable animal aunts and I was incredibly fortunate to unearth some absolute gems who also turned out to be wonderful with children.

There was a girl whose name was Sonia, who came from Yorkshire. Sophie was about 13 years old at the time and was going through a pyromaniac phase, setting her Barbie dolls on fire. As you do. Sophie had managed to acquire a number of cigarette lighters – don't ask me how. Anyway, Sonia simply said to her: "Right then Sophie, give me all your lighters." And she did. Sonia was also great with horses, and one of the things that I have discovered on my journey through life is that girls who are good with horses are almost always good with teenagers because they treat them both the same. These girls are used to dealing with a horse that is much bigger and stronger than they are, so it stands to reason that they are not going to be phased by a teenage girl or boy.

"You've just got to treat them right," Sonia would say. "Give them food at the right time, talk to them with a firm voice and keep them in a routine and they will be fine with you." I could never quite figure out

Mum and Dad were a photogenic couple

Dad, far right, with his brothers, Maurice, who died in a motor torpedo attack during the second world war, and Tony, who became a tea planter

Dad in his days at Winchester

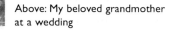

Above: My beloved grandmother at a wedding

Left: Granny makes sure I look my best for the camera

With Mum and Bella the dog

My first TV role, left, in *Jesus of Nazareth*

Above: Clancy goes looking for
the head ranger in an early
episode of *Skippy*

Right: With Mark Hammond
(Ken James), Matt Hammond
(Ed Devereaux) and Sonny
(Garry Pankhurst) around
the breakfast table in *Skippy*

Above: Genuine Aborigines appeared in
Skippy and I soon learnt how poorly
treated they were by the Australians

Right: Wombats look so cute and cuddly,
and then they go and blow up a mine shaft

Above: Not exactly my
favourite bedfellow –
a co-star in *Seal Morning*

left: That's my boy!
With Thom, aged three

Right: One of my favourite
pictures of Thom, taken
when he has 18 months old

Mummy's boy. Looking impossibly young
with my new baby son

With Judy, one of my canine co-stars in *Woof*

My mentor, the amazing Phil Gardner

Above: With Alan Ayckbourn, who is,
quite simply, a genius

Left: Was there ever a funnier man than
my old friend Christopher Biggins?

On the set of *Mr Pastry* – that's me on Mousey, second left

Life's a beach. In Cornwall with my sister and her daughter, Alice

Man's best friend. A selection of the dogs that have brought me so much joy

Above: Daughter Sophie with Bebe, another of our dogs

Left: We had so many great dogs in *Woof*, and Punch was one of the best

My gentle giant. David with Spade,
the star of *Tarka The Otter*

Thom and Sophie help David and I to celebrate our
wedding day – the dog was a bridesmaid

The adorable Puppy Wuppy

Above: Thom and his wife Leanne
with Oscar, my grandson

Left: Adelaide, my wonderful
grand-daughter, who thought I
could really fly

An unguarded moment on the set of Midsomer Murders, with John Nettles in the background

Above: Like me, Adelaide caught the riding bug early. Here she is on Starlight, her pony

Left: Where it all began. The land Down Under – with my parents and sister in Sydney, not long after our big move

My daughter Sophie

There are times when, even though
I say so myself, I still scrub up
pretty well for a pensioner
Photos: Stephen Rainer

whether she was talking about horses or teenagers. She never once raised her voice, but everybody always did what she said, without question.

CHAPTER 18
THE GENTLE GIANT

"I met David for lunch and made sure that I got there early because I wanted to create a good impression because I was well aware of the quality of the work he had produced up to that point."

Sometimes, to go forwards with a story, it is necessary to backtrack, and I hope you will forgive me for doing that now, as I explain my relationship with David Cobham, which started off as director-actor, and eventually grew into something rather more than that.

David had produced and directed *Tarka the Otter*, an amazing film based on the novel by Henry Williamson. He co-wrote the film script with Williamson and Gerald Durrell, the naturalist, zookeeper, conservationist, author and television presenter – a man of many, many talents. Speaking of which, it was narrated by the remarkable Peter Ustinov and it starred an otter called Spade.

David had also just won a Bafta for *Amundsen*, which told the story of the Norwegian explorer Roald Amundsen, who battled against the odds to lead the first expedition to the South Pole. He was the man who, in 1911, beat Captain Scott to the Pole by a month. He had set out in 1910 with sufficient provisions for two years and took with him nearly 100

Greenland sled dogs. He had originally planned to tackle the North Pole but had to change his plans when he was beaten to it.

His ship headed south, without any of the crew knowing where they were going until they had been at sea for a month. When they reached land, on 14 January, 1911, they struck camp and began preparations for their marathon journey. They had arrived in the middle of the Antarctic winter and could do nothing until conditions improved – at that time of year it is dark for most of the day. Eventually the weather improved sufficiently to allow the mission to begin and Amundsen set off with a team of eight men and sledges pulled by 86 dogs. But the weather turned, and Amundsen and his team had to call off their first attempt and return to camp.

In the end, a team of five men headed off, each with a sledge pulled by 13 dogs. They lived off seal meat and blubber and survived some atrocious weather, constantly fighting against blizzards and the fear that Scott had beaten them to it. But they got there first and Amundsen managed to get all his men safely back to base camp, although they did lose several dogs along the way. It was a remarkable story of courage and man's ability to overcome adversity.

Tarka wasn't David's first wildlife film – he was also responsible for *The Goshawk*, *To Build a Fire* and *Survival in Limbo*, but *Tarka* was his most famous work and after he made it he became pretty hot property. As a result, in 1980 he was given *Brendon Chase*, a 13-part series by Southern Television with what was in those days an astronomical budget of more than £1m.

The subject matter was children and animals, and was right up his street, so he had very little hesitation in accepting it. In Watkins-Pitchford's original novel, journalist Monica Hurling played a minor role, but James Andrew Hall, who adapted the book for television, told David that he was certain he could something with the character if he was allowed to expand it.

David tells the story that he was speaking to his agent before the show was cast, and apparently his agent said to him: "Right then David, you have some great scripts here and this is a great opportunity, but you have got to go for first XI actors. I am certain this is going to be a success. Perhaps Liza Goddard might be interested in playing Monica Hurling. You lose nothing by asking her."

He asked his agent to get in touch with me and to 'put in a good word'. Two weeks later we met for lunch at a restaurant in Pimlico Road – I made sure that I got there early because I wanted to create a good impression on David because I was well aware of the quality of the work he had produced up to that point. The first thing that struck me when he walked in was his height – he stood 6ft 7in but, like so many tall people, he turned out to be a gentle giant of a man.

And I was only too happy to accept the part, proving once again how incredibly lucky I have been throughout my career because, once again, it was a role that landed in my lap without me having to go out and fight for it.

And, of course, he assembled a wonderful cast. I got to work with a whole host of incredible actors, many of whom were extraordinary characters.

One of my co-stars in *Brendon Chase* was Jimmy Edwards, famous for programmes such as *Whacko*, and also for his handlebar moustache. Jimmy really was a larger than life character.

I remember being on set one morning at about 7am and David had a polystyrene cup full of coffee in his hand. Jimmy appeared and said:

134

"Blimey David, that looks a bit hot. Let me sort it out for you." With that, he reached into his pocket, produced a hip flask and proceeded to pour a very generous measure of brandy into David's cup. At seven in the morning!

Jimmy played a huntsman and although he had been a fine rider in his time, he insisted on being given a quiet horse for the part.

I quickly discovered that one of David's great strengths as a director was his warmth and his ability to empathise with actors and get the best from them without bullying them. Some directors are fearful bullies.

Brendon Chase was set in the 1920s. It told the story of three brothers (Robin, John and Harold Hensman) who spend eight months living as outlaws and go to live in the forest of Brendon Chase.

Their mother had died and their father was living and working in India, leaving them to be cared for by their Aunt Ellen, a strict and somewhat cold spinster. At the end of the Easter holidays, Harold falls ill with the measles, so Robin and John are unable to return to boarding school. They decide to run away and fend for themselves, taking some food from their aunt's house, and also taking a rifle and ammunition so they can survive in the wild.

Despite continued attempts to catch them (usually involving Police Sergeant Bunting and the Reverend Whiting, played in by Christopher Biggins) the brothers prove sufficiently quick-witted to evade capture for eight months, surviving on what they can kill (the acceptance of which is one of the most interesting aspects of both the book and the TV series today) and on supplies occasionally taken from other sources.

My character was a cynical journalist called Monica Hurling of The London Planet newspaper, who has written a number of stories stirring up public interest in the Hensman boys, while the paper has offered a

£50 reward to whoever can find them.

In the later part of their time living in the wild, the boys - who by this time have long been wearing rabbit skins, their clothes having worn out - encounter an eccentric elderly charcoal burner called Smokoe Joe who becomes a close friend. When Smokoe Joe is seriously injured, one of the boys saves his life by running for the doctor, thereby risking capture. After a Christmas spent with Smokoe Joe in his hut, the boys are 'run to ground' when the doctor, who has kept their secret until that moment, arrives with their father who has returned, and the story ends there in the forest. The bear that had escaped in the forest near the end of their adventure settles down to hibernate for the winter in the hollow oak tree where they had lived.

The series was filmed mainly around the New Forest, with music by Paul Lewis, and it contained some striking wildlife photography. Apart from Britain, it was also shown in Germany, Holland, Sweden and Norway.

My character had several scenes where she had to fly in a biplane; unfortunately, because of insurance, the producers wouldn't let me in the plane, and replaced me with a dummy. On reflection, it probably wasn't such a bad thing because the plane had various bolts missing and we all admired the pilot who flew it.

I met Biggins for the first time on the set of *Brendon Chase*. One day he was filming a scene in which he had to drive along in the old convertible car owned his character and the scene called for the plane, supposedly flown by Monica, to buzz the car. David briefed the pilot beforehand and said: "See if you can actually touch down on the road just behind the car and then carry on over the car – that would be great if you could manage to pull that off." The pilot said he would do his best, but I don't think any of us truly believed he could do it because we all knew it was both tricky and dangerous.

David and his crew were filming the scene on a long lens, about 100 yards away from where this was due to happen, and the pilot did it on the first take. It was astonishing. Biggins, on the other hand, was not as impressed as the rest of us as the plane flew over the car, missing his head by inches. He ended up shaking his fist at David.

The programme also featured a bear, which was an integral part of the whole story. David had previously worked with a chap called John Irvine on the *Explorer* series that had included the Amundsen film. John had worked on a version of Dickens' *Hard Times* and had used a bear in the production, so David called him to ask whether it was as tame and manageable as it had appeared to be.

John assured him that it was and told him to go to Coventry zoo, so off he went and was taken into a large room and was told to sit down. A couple of minutes later, the bear came into the room with its handler and sat down on a chair opposite David. The handler then gave the bear a pipe, lit it and the animal sat there puffing away on the pipe. He asked the handler what else it did and was told that it would do just about anything.

The first day I came on set, David said to me: "Come on Liza, come and meet the bear."

And there was this enormous brown bear with a chain round its neck. The chain was attached to a tree trunk that had been lying on the ground, but as I approached the bear he was tossing this log around as if it were a twig.

We had a wonderful actor called Michael Robbins and there was a scene that called for him to be chased up a tree by the bear. Michael told us that he couldn't climb trees, but when the bear went after him I had never in my life seen an actor move so quickly. The bear then followed him up the tree – around its neck was some clear fishing line, so fine that it didn't show up on camera. How anybody thought they could ever control this magnificent animal with a piece of fishing line I will never know. If the mood had taken it, the bear would have snapped the line in the blink of an eye, and that is more or less what happened because as he climbed the tree, the line became caught up in the branches and started pulling at his neck. Naturally, he didn't like it, so he broke it and ran off into the New Forest.

So we now had a situation where there was a frightened bear running around in the New Forest. We phoned the police, and there was a stunned silence on the other end of the phone, broken only when the officer said: "Oh dear. We have a party of boy scouts doing an orienteering course in the New Forest today." Then they had the task of getting officers into the New Forest to get the boys out, and they were accompanied by a police marksman who was ready to shoot the bear because obviously you can't have a bear rampaging around in a forest that is used and enjoyed by members of the public.

The bear was owned by a couple who lived with it in a caravan and they found him before the marksman did. He was sound asleep under a tree – the grand adventure had all been too much for him. Fortunately, it was tame and was generally pretty well behaved.

For much of the time that we were filming the weather was extremely cold, and its handlers used to say how lucky they were to be able to bunk down at night in their trailer with the bear because it kept them warm. I believe it may even have been house trained.

The bear also featured in what could be described as the money shot of the entire series. There were two paths in the New Forest that came together and David managed to get a shot of one of the boys walking down one path playing a flute, with the bear walking down the other, attracted by the sound of the music, and they both reached the point where the two paths became one at the same time. Brilliant stuff.

There is an interesting postscript to the Michael Robbins story – the scene called for him to wear a cape and a helmet and although it didn't hamper his efforts to climb up the tree, getting back down was a different matter altogether because the helmet obscured his view so he was unable to look down properly, with the result that he kept landing in a heap and falling over. It was a miracle that he didn't break any bones.

Years later, I worked with Jimmy Edwards again when we starred in a Ray Cooney play together. He had just come back from Australia after somebody outed him as being gay. In those days, if it was discovered that you were homosexual it destroyed your career. After the story broke in the English press, poor Jimmy fled to Australia, where he lived for some years.

It would barely cause anybody to raise an eyebrow now, but it was a big deal in the 1940s, '50s and '60s. Men were meant to be real men, and their women were supposed to know. Rock Hudson was probably the most famous example of a big Hollywood star who kept his sexuality private because he knew only too well that if came out that he was gay then his acting career would be in ruins.

One day I walked past Jimmy in the theatre.

"Hello Jim, how are you?"

"I am completely pissed Liza."

Somehow, he managed to get himself on stage and get through the

139

show. Back in the day, people turned a blind eye. As long as the actor in question didn't let people down, they were allowed to get away with it.

Temptation was never far away – apart from the theatre bars, I have worked in theatres where there were bars beside the stage. That was never a good idea. And there are countless stories about actors walking into pubs in full costume and downing a couple of pints of beer or a couple of shots of whisky before going on stage.

Journalists used to have a bit of a reputation for enjoying their drink, and I remember meeting Jeffrey Bernard, the hard-drinking journalist and columnist – he was sprawled on a sofa and was so drunk that I couldn't understand a word he was saying. He was off his trolley. It was very funny, but it was also very sad. One of his adoring coterie said to me: "Be careful, he marries actresses." I looked at this man in utter astonishment. Did he really think that I would ever want to marry this shrivelled hulk of a man. Keith Waterhouse wrote a play, *Jeffrey Barnard is Unwell*, which chronicled his life story – and the consumption of alcohol featured large.

I don't drink alcohol. There are no sinister reasons. It is simply that it has never really agreed with me. When I was young and growing up in Australia, I tried it, but every time I had more than a couple of drinks I would throw up all over the place, whether it be at home, over the stairs, in friends' houses. It was horrible, and I figured that somebody was trying to tell me something, namely that I had a very low tolerance level for alcohol.

I used to drink the odd glass of champagne, for birthdays and Christmas and suchlike, and wine with meals, but now I don't touch a drop. To be honest, I don't even like the smell of alcohol now. Instead, I prefer to work out in the gym and do what has to be done to keep fit.

Acting can be a physically demanding profession, so it is important to stay in shape.

When I was starring in the Ayckbourn plays in Scarborough during 2010, a couple of members of the cast were smokers, and I am not too thrilled to admit that I started again, having kicked the habit some years before. I knew that when I got home to Norfolk I could stop straight away – and I did. People will ask why I would ever start again in the first place, and the answer is simple enough. I enjoy the occasional cigarette.

When I gave up, I did so without the help of patches, gum or anything else. I have a friend who quit smoking ten years ago with the help of nicotine gum – the problem is that that person is now addicted to the gum, and has been for ten years, and I reckon that probably does more harm than the cigarettes. Willpower is the only thing that works for me.

CHAPTER 19
SEAL MORNING

"We had some problems with the seals. They may look cute and cuddly but the thing with seals is that they bite, they have sharp teeth and very strong jaws."

I worked for David again in 1985 on a series called *Seal Morning*, which featured an American called David Birney, who was a big star back then. He had appeared in many marquee television series, including *St Elsewhere*, *Serpico* and *Valley of the Dolls*, and was a distinguished stage actor whose credits include *Hamlet*, *Romeo and Juliet*, *To Kill a Mockingbird*, *The Importance of Being Earnest*, *Camelot*, *My Fair Lady* and *As You Like It*.

When he arrived on the set of *Seal Morning*, right from the off he played the part of the big Hollywood actor. Jane Lapotaire had an argument with him in which she told him that he was just an arsehole, and after that he was absolutely fine.

Before a take, English actors will wait patiently until they hear the director say: "Action." And then, off we go and act out the scene until we hear the director say: "Cut." Many of the Americans, however, will stand and complain about how cold they feel or whatever, making it impossible for both themselves and their fellow actors to hear anything that the director might have to say. Birney fell into that category.

One of the central characters had a pet rat, and the character I played was required to scream when she saw it – I screamed so loudly that the sound recordist almost fell off his perch.

We had some problems with the seals. They may look cute and cuddly but the thing with seals is that they bite, they have sharp teeth and very strong jaws. You had to be very careful that they didn't bite your finger off, thinking it is a fish. Julian Fellowes nearly lost his fingers, having been told by David not to stroke them with his fingers protruding – the secret was to make a fist, but Julian was filming a scene and he forgot. As he moved his fingers towards the seal's head it opened its jaws and was just about to close them on Julian's fingers when he pulled them back. It was just in the nick of time too – if he hadn't got them out of them way you can take it from me that he would have lost his fingers, and we wouldn't have enjoyed *Downton Abbey*. You learn valuable lessons from incidents like that and never take things for granted.

Seal Morning was about an orphaned girl and her lonely aunt living in 1930s' England who attract the attention of a handsome naturalist when they decide to raise an abandoned seal. Lapotaire, one of our best actresses, starred as a ferocious aunt.

The series was my first experience of Norfolk and it was entirely dependent upon the weather. We used to get up each day and pray that it was dry so that we could film the outdoor scenes because if it was raining we were forced inside to do interior shots. It was one of the wettest summers I had ever experienced – it seemed to pour with rain day after day. It was relentless and we ended up doing hundreds of interior scenes, waiting for a break in the weather. It was incredibly frustrating.

At one point I turned up every day for two weeks to do an outside shot, and every day I was told that I wasn't going to be needed because it was so wet and miserable. One day there was a break in the weather, so we all piled into the vehicles and headed off to the reedbeds. David looked skywards and said: "Right, I think we are going to be all right. It is clearing." And as he spoke, there was a huge clap of thunder and the rain came down in stair-rods. In our haste to get away, somebody drove one of the Land Rovers into a ditch.

CHAPTER 20
CHILD'S PLAY

"Every time poor Lionel went anywhere near the bear, it spat at him. And we had to erect electric fences round the set to prevent it from running away."

My first two marriages were mistakes. I admit it, and I can look back now and say that I learnt some valuable lessons.

After my split with Alvin, I went out on a few dates, but nothing serious. I am not going to tell you that I had been put off marriage for life because that simply wouldn't be true. I still believed, deep down, that if I ever met the right man then there might still be a chance for me, although half of me also wondered whether I was really cut out for marriage.

My career was taking a whole new direction, and I found myself doing increasing amounts of children's television, including Play School, *Playaway* and *Jackanory*. I had a marvellous time. Why so much of this type of work came my way I really don't know, although I suppose it might well have been because of my time on *Skippy*.

I must have made some kind of impression on David because when he came to make *Woof!*, I was given another part. *Woof!* was about the adventures of a boy who turns into a dog, based on a book by Allan

Ahlberg. It was directed by David and written by Richard Fegen and Andrew Norriss.

When it came to putting *Woof!* together, David's executive producer, Lewis Rudd, said to him: "David, there are all these wonderful, top-quality, middle-aged actresses out there grumbling about not getting any work. Why not try Penelope Keith and see if she will do an episode?" He called Penelope and, sure enough, she accepted the part offered to her without hesitation. After that, we had no trouble attracting talent into each new series, including the likes of Anita Dobson, Nigel Havers, Anthony Head, Leslie Phillips, Leslie Grantham and Stephen Fry.

The show was first broadcast in 1989 and I played Mrs Jessop, a teacher who had an inkling about what was going on, but was never able to get conclusive proof. Edward Fidoe played Eric Banks, the boy who turned into a dog and also starred Thomas Aldwinckle as Eric's friend Roy Ackerman and later Sarah Smart as his tomboy best friend Rachel Hobbs.

The show generally featured weekly escapades to do with the dog's power. Late in Eric's run of episodes, he discovered that the transition was caused by adrenalin, and met up with an adult (played by Anthony Head), who had the same affliction.

The story was always about Eric keeping his secret from both his parents and his headmaster (the late John Ringham), who was always plagued by a dog that kept coming into the school – that dog, of course, was Eric.

From series six which began airing in 1993, the episodes featured the adventures of Rex Thomas (played by Adam Roper) and his best friend Michael Tully (Monty Allen). Rex inherited Eric's condition, and later became Mrs Jessop's stepson after my character married his father, Ken

(Owen Brennan). Lionel Jeffries also featured as Rex's grandfather, and Leslie Grantham appeared in some later episodes as Mr Garrett, a ruthless dog warden. I got to work with Stephen Fry in one episode - he played a cartoonist.

You will remember that I told you about the bear in *Brendon Chase*, and how tame it was. When we were filming *Woof!*, there was an episode that featured another bear, and the plot called for a scene where it was together with Jeffries. Let's just say that this bear had an entirely different temperament to the other one, and although we had been assured that it was tame, it really wasn't. Every time poor Lionel went anywhere near the animal, it spat at him. And we had to erect electric fences round the set to prevent it from running away.

In this day and age, health and safety regulations would never allow such a thing to happen, for the sake of both the animal and the cast and crew. And, of course, it is possible to do such marvellous things with special effects that you could probably shoot the whole thing without the need for a real bear to be anywhere near the set. But back then, we had no choice, and putting somebody in a bear costume really wasn't an option either, not if you wanted your audience to believe what they were seeing.

One of the things that may surprise you about Jeffries was that, although myself and the other actors got along just fine with him, he was a very difficult person for the production crew to work with, and David really didn't enjoy directing him. If you ever watched him on screen, he always came across like everybody's favourite grandfather.

When you have an actor appearing with a dog, one of the key things that has to happen is for the actor to go out of his or her way to establish a relationship with the dog and win its trust and affection, and Lionel refused to do that. If it came anywhere near him, he would tell it to go away. He also frustrated the writers hugely because he had this habit of taking the script away and rewriting it in such a way that he always had the final line. But he was somebody who could act everybody else off the screen.

David wanted him to appear in another series, but not for every episode, and his response was: "I am either going to be in every one or I am not going to appear in at all." And so he never came back.

The ninth and final series, consisting of seven episodes, aired in 1997. It featured Jim Walters (Sebastian Mahjouri, accompanied by his cousin Brian Barford (Jack Allen) and next door neighbour Carrie Howard (Faye Jackson). By the time the show ended, I was the only original cast member left. Four dogs were used over the years.

Early episodes were filmed around the suburb of Moseley in Birmingham. Later, production moved to Nottingham. Apart from Britain, it was also broadcast in Australia, and it turned out to be Carlton's biggest-selling series of the time.

The whole concept was brilliant, and David and his writers thought of everything – when you watch Superman go into a phone booth and emerge in his cape, do you never wonder what has happened to his clothes? I know that I do. When the boy turned into the dog, the problem was always that he still had his clothes, so he needed to have his best friend with him, and his best friend needed to have a bag into which he could put the clothes. And then, when he turned back from the boy into a boy, there was the problem in reverse, so his friend would have to hide him until he could get some clothes, and they also used to leave items of clothing hidden in various places.

We had four incredible dogs. Pippin was the first and was a very famous TV dog.

The second dog was called Judy, and looked exactly like Pippin. She was an extraordinary animal, whose only reward was to have a ball thrown for her.

Just in case you are wondering why we went through so many boys, the answer is fairly simple – puberty. They outgrew the part, their voices broke and had to be replaced. One of the more comical aspects of this was David at 6ft 7in, having to take the boys to one side and say to them: "I am sorry but you have got too big so we are going to have to find somebody else."

They would look up at him and say: "We are too big?" And then there would be tears. It was awful.

The next dog was Punch, who was found in a rescue centre in Birmingham. His trainer would make hand signals for him. For instance, if she held her fist up once, it would signify that she wanted him to bark once, if she held her fist up twice it meant she wanted two barks, and so on. It was possible to have long dialogue sequences with this remarkable animal, who was the most intelligent dog I have ever come across.

We forgot that he was a dog. In fact, on one occasion David famously walked up to him and started giving him instructions.

And the next dog was called Tinker, once again brought in with a new group of boys to replace the ones who had outgrown their parts. It was a great series that brought joy to a lot people – in fact, it was the first daytime programme to win an Emmy in America, so it had to be good because they don't hand those out for fun. David went over for the ceremony, never thinking for a moment that he would win, so you can imagine how he felt when they did.

Woof! was a Carlton TV production, and back in 1985 I appeared in a production of *Roll over Beethoven*, which was the first to be filmed in their new studios in Nottingham – while we were filming, the builders were still trying to finish the place off, and there was a constant hammering going on in the background.

The *Woof!* years were wonderful, some of the happiest of my professional career, but in 1992 I was shattered by the death of my beloved father, who died after suffering a heart attack at the age of 67. I felt that I had been cheated – he was far too young to die and I had wanted him to have time to enjoy both his grandchildren, to see them growing up. Losing Dad was a devastating blow, and one that I struggled to get over. Throwing myself into my work was one of the ways that I managed to cope.

After *Woof!*, David and I worked together from 1996 until 1998 on *Out of Sight*. A 12-year-old boy genius discovers an experiment in an old diary and a copy of *The Invisible Man* by HG Wells. With the help of a friend he recreates the experiment and makes a substance to turn people and things invisible by simply spraying it with the trademark green-bottled solution. The effects were reverted, whether intentional or not, by the appliance of water. It was hugely popular with children, largely because most kids long to be invisible sometimes. When you think about it, it would be the perfect way to get up to all sorts of mischief.

And then there was *Bernard's Watch*. I played the part of the narrator in the first run of the series, which went from 1997 until 2001. It was about a young boy called Bernard who was always late, until a postman gave him a 'magic watch' which could stop time. He soon found out that the postman had magical powers, and that these watches were given to people who needed them. The rules of him keeping his watch were that he couldn't use it to commit crimes and couldn't be greedy.

Every episode focused on Bernard or someone he'd lent the watch to facing a problem or simply doing day-to-day stuff and trying to sort it out, using the watch. It began as a single 15-minute episode, but it was suggested it would work as a series. Four more stories were written by creator Andrew Norriss, who thought, in his own words, "that would be it". He ended up writing six entire series.

I haven't a clue why it is that I have ended up doing so many children's television programmes. It was certainly never part of my great career plan, but I have to admit that, without exception, they have been enormous fun to do.

CHAPTER 21
THIRD TIME LUCKY

"We were married in 1994 and this time there was no doubt in my mind. I was certain that I was making the correct decision. And I have been proved to be absolutely right."

Through spending so much time working together, David and I became very good friends, and we'd shared many dinners together while on the set of all the shows I have told you about. It meant that we got to know one another really well and we realised that we had a great deal in common.

After Alvin, I was on my own for around five years – I had some boyfriends in that time, but none of the relationships came to anything. I was single and then David's marriage broke down.

During the filming of *Woof!* David had asked me home a couple of times at weekends, and had behaved impeccably. We had gone out bird watching, eaten big meals and talked and talked and talked. At the end of one series, David told me he had given Anita Dobson a goodbye, thank-you hug and had told her she had a lovely bum. I said nothing, but a few days later I wrote David a letter and finished it off by telling him that he could feel my bum anytime he fancied. The die was cast.

He moved in with me to my cottage in Surrey and, gradually, Thom and Sophie accepted him. They could see that he made me happy.

As you will have concluded, it is extremely difficult to keep a relationship going if you work in the acting profession, and especially so if one partner is an actor and the other is in no way connected with acting. Despite my experiences, I believe you have the best chance of making a relationship work if you are both involved in the business because at least then you develop an understanding of what your partner might be going through, and you accept that part and parcel of the job is being away from home, sometimes for very long periods.

In the past, things were actually at their best when I lived and worked in and around London because at least it meant that I could come home to my own bed every night, and I still had the energy to sit down and catch up on the day's events. It was much, much more difficult when I lived in the country and worked in the West End because I wasn't getting home until midnight – and that was six days a week.

Early in our relationship I was touring in George Bernard Shaw's *Candida*, and David used to join me whenever he could. We were playing in Inverness and he told me that he wanted me to meet his cousin Susannah, who lived in Elgin, and that he also wanted to take me to the Isle of Skye.

David hired a Fiat Punto and we were on Sky in no time, had a quick tour round the island, enjoyed lunch together and then started back. The A887 to Inverness from Skye is at time narrow, with storm drains on either side of the road. We noticed three sheep on the right-hand side of the Fiat, and there was a car coming in the opposite direction. Two of the sheep leapt across the road, while the third stopped right in the middle. David had no option but to hit it. It was awful – the bonnet flew up and, for a brief time that seemed to last an eternity, he was driving blind. Eventually we came to a halt and the bonnet flopped down again. Somehow he had managed to steer a straight line – if he hadn't, we would surely have plunged to our deaths.

The car was a write-off but the driver of the other car had stopped, so he took us to a nearby fish farm, where there was a phone. My big concern was getting back to the theatre before the curtain went up that evening, but the AA assured us that they would send somebody and, sure enough, I made it back in the nick of time.

David and I got together properly in about 1993 and we were married in 1994 while we were making *Woof!* together. This time there was no doubt in my mind. I was certain that I was making the correct decision. And I have been proved to be absolutely right. David is the gentle man that I thought he was. He is a loving and caring individual and the years I have spent with him have been incredibly happy.

He is also a font of ideas – they just come gushing out, and when we first started living together the two of us would sit down and throw suggestions at each other; we used to take the better ideas to the point of getting a script together and then presenting it to various television companies, but it became increasingly difficult to get them to develop any new project. I haven't a clue how anything that is different and innovative gets off the ground these days because everybody seems to be so cautious, so frightened to take a chance. But unless you take chances, how will you ever know if something is going to work?

When we got married I sold my house in Surrey and bought a place in Norfolk, and so began my love affair with the county. I had fallen in love with Norfolk the first time I saw, so it was no hardship to move my children, my dogs and my horse.

This may sound daft, but in so many ways it reminds me of Australia – I think it is the big skies. You either love it or hate it. And then there are the huge beaches, miles and miles of golden sand with nobody on them. One of my most treasured memories is of Sophie and I riding our horses on Holkham beach.

I consider myself to be very lucky to have found that somebody special to share my life with. I have friends who have gone through divorce and never seem to have recovered or got over the bitterness of it all – when you feel bitter, it makes it so much more difficult to move on with your life.

CHAPTER 22
DICING WITH DEATH

"I am a great believer in the power of the mind – if you believe that something terrible is going to happen, then it probably will. If, on the other hand, you believe that something wonderful is going to happen to you, then you increase the chances of making that happen too."

In 1997 I was diagnosed with breast cancer. I had discovered a lump but was in no discomfort. Nevertheless, I wasted no time in seeing my doctor, who immediately referred me to the hospital. Like most people, I worried what they might find, but tried to put it to the back of mind and convince myself that it would be nothing. I was told at the hospital that 90% of such lumps turned out to be cysts. And it turned out that mine was a cyst. The relief was enormous.

But not long afterwards, I found another lump. By this time I was certain that it would also turn out to be a cyst. But mine wasn't a cyst, and when the diagnosis came back, it was like a bolt from the blue.

Naturally, you initially think the worst – I believe that is human nature. And then you make up your mind that you are going to beat it. You do lots of research and read everything you can, and I realised that it is treatable and that most women recover and go on to live perfectly normal lives.

I had a lumpectomy, during which they removed the lump and I went away thinking that everything would be fine. Unfortunately, it didn't quite turn out that way and I got a phone call telling me they hadn't got it all and that I should come back and see the oncologist. He explained to me that I had two options – I could leave it alone and they would keep an eye on it, which is the choice I would make now, or radiotherapy, which was the route I chose.

I am convinced that the radiotherapy made the condition worse. I now wish that we had left it alone and monitored it as I believe that all we succeeded in doing was aggravating it.

For six weeks I underwent radiotherapy, five days a week. I had been told that it was a breeze so I went into it with that attitude, and I sailed through it. You hear all sorts of horror stories, but I managed to cope just fine. I am a great believer in the power of the mind – if you believe that something terrible is going to happen, then it probably will. If, on the other hand, you believe that something wonderful is going to happen to you, then you increase the chances of making that happen too.

Some people react very badly to radiotherapy, but I was quite fortunate. I would sometimes wake up in the middle of the night with a burning sensation and would have to apply cold water to my skin to cool it down, but apart from that I felt absolutely fine. There were no side effects at all.

In fact, I felt so well that after having five days of treatment during the week, I was able to film a delightful series for Anglia Television called *Liza's Country* at the weekend. It was such a thrill. I enjoyed it tremendously and I am immensely proud of it.

I did the programme for three years with a marvellous producer called Alison Starsmore who found all sorts of extraordinary people and unusual events for us to look at. For instance, we went to a truck festival at Peterborough – who would ever have thought that such a thing would exist? My claim to fame with that was that I got to interview Eddie Stobart. Although his company was featured in a series during 2010, Eddie did not appear in it, and he never gives interviews, so I am especially proud of the fact that he talked to me. And he was another wonderful man, with a passion for the work that he and his company do. I even ended up with a Stobart truck with my name emblazoned on the front – all his company's trucks are named after women, and the drivers treat them with great affection. I suppose it is only natural that they would because they spend so much time in the cab.

I did an assault course with the Marines, and I can tell you for nothing that they made no allowances for me being a woman. And I flew in a biplane with a man who asked if I wanted to loop the loop. I said no, so of course he went ahead and did it anyway. My screams could be heard all over Norfolk. At that moment when we were upside down, I realised that the only thing that was holding me in was my harness.

Believe it or believe it not, but I met a man who had the biggest collection of knots in Britain. There were times when it was difficult to keep my face straight, but these people are so passionate about what they do that you end up being swept along with it all. I had worked on another series called *Collector's Lot* which also featured people who collected things, so I was used to the enthusiasm they all possessed.

It was all done off the cuff. I used to take one of my dogs with me, a shih tzu-Yorkshire terrier cross called Puppy Wuppy, and that always helped to break the ice. Then we would just sit down and chat, seeing how it would all develop.

With the knot man, all that I had to do was say: "Tell me about your knots..." And off he went. I didn't know there were all sorts of knots, did you? For instance, there are specific knots used only by sailors. As long as the people you are talking to feel that you are interested in what they have to say, then you will get the best out of them, and I have always been a very good listener. If you put on a front, they will see straight through you.

I also tried my hand at barge painting. There are few things more spectacular than a beautifully decorated barge, and I got to see one close up and personal. We did another programme about Dedham Mill and its link with the artist John Constable.

Alison found all these people, and I think one of the reasons the series worked so well was because we had such a small crew. There was myself, a cameraman, a soundman, Alison and my dog, and that was it. We became like a small family.

The beauty of the series for me was that it was filmed all over East Anglia, so I always knew that I would be able to get home at night.

After doing *Liza's Country*, nothing should have surprised me, but I did a double take when the producers of *Collector's Lot* told me that I was going to meet a man who collected gas cookers. I thought they were winding me up.

But when we got there, his entire house was full of them – they were in the hall, up the stairs, in the bedrooms, and the only one that worked was the one in the kitchen. We had difficulty moving around because there were so many. You will not be surprised to learn that there was no woman in his life, but this man was passionate about his cookers.

Then there was the man who was the world's greatest authority on string. Can you imagine it? Apart from anything else, how does one become the world's greatest authority on string?

One episode that we did at Chatsworth House stands out. We were going to film in the greenhouses on the estate and it was the middle of winter, but I thought that the greenhouses would be boiling hot. I arrived wearing summer clothes, only to discover that nobody had told me that what we were actually going to be filming were the remains of the greenhouses at Chatsworth. The thing that made them unique was that they had been designed by the same man who designed the greenhouses for the Great Exhibition.

I have never been so cold in my entire life.

I met some remarkable people during that period of my life. I also met some individuals who were quite, quite batty, and the one who springs to mind immediately is Chris Eubank, the former world boxing champion, who lived in Brighton.

At the time, he lived in a massive house and also owned another smaller house that contained his state-of-the-art gym and changing rooms. This guy was a true eccentric, although he was charming.

We arrived in the morning, as arranged, but he told us that he wasn't ready for us and told us to go in to his office and wait for him. I believe he regarded himself as being on a par with royalty and that he would only receive people when he was good and ready to do so. The reason he was late was because he spent so long getting dressed, making himself look perfect before appearing in front of the camera.

His office came as something of a surprise because laid out neatly were 90 pairs of shoes. He had a butler, a former soldier, and part of his job was to polish Eubank's shoes. We had come to look at his collection of walking sticks and canes, but I said to the director: "This is what is interesting – this is the real story. People will love to see this." And the director agreed.

But we had to go through the motions with his walking sticks. When Eubank finally appeared he was dressed immaculately, and was wearing a monocle.

As I have already said, with most people, all that I would to do was say: "Right then, tell us all about your walking sticks..." And off they would go, telling me what they were made of, where they had picked them up, how much they were worth, what had got them interested in the first place. Chris Eubank, however, was not 'most people'.

To kick things off, I asked him how many walking sticks he had, expecting him to say that he owned hundreds. His reply? "I've got six."

In anybody's language, six walking sticks did not constitute a collection.

"Six? You've got six walking sticks?"

I asked if we could see them and he duly returned and set down his six walking sticks. It was absolutely hopeless. I knew it, the director knew it, the cameraman knew it and, deep down, I suspect that even Eubank knew it.

I tried to soldier on. "Tell me about your walking sticks Chris."

"Oh I can't really remember. I will need to phone the man I buy them from."

This was not at all helpful. Anyway, he then had to phone his antique dealer, who was based in London, and get the lowdown on all the sticks. But I would ask him a question and he wouldn't have a clue what the answer was, so he would have to phone the dealer again. And there behind him were 90 pairs of gleaming shoes, most of which appeared to have been hand-made, and about which he would almost certainly have known everything.

Somehow we managed to get a programme out of it, with much hilarity. With somebody like Chris Eubank, you could hardly go wrong.

Before he lost all his money and was declared bankrupt, Eubank was obsessive about his appearance and spent a fortune on his clothes. Just about the only thing he had left at the end of it all was a truck that he used to drive around Brighton.

In the meantime, I thought that I had beaten the cancer but in 2000 I had a mammogram and they discovered that it had actually spread and things did not look good. The year 2000 was a massive one for me in several ways – I started off the year working with the beloved Christopher Biggins in *Lady Windermere's Fan*, which I had first appeared in way back in 1971. It was a blissful time, mainly thanks to Biggins – I laughed from nine in the morning, when we would meet for breakfast, until one o'clock the following morning when we all stagger off to our rooms having been out for a meal with Biggins' friends. He has friends everywhere.

During that tour, Adelaide, my grand-daughter was born on 9 March and I was the first person to hold her, and fell madly in love with her right there and then.

Then we finished the tour and I had one option and one option only, and that was to have a mastectomy and reconstruction in October. I didn't especially care for my oncologist in Norfolk – he was good enough at his job, but I didn't like his bedside manner at all, so I took the decision to have the surgery performed in London.

I contacted Breakthrough Cancer, for whom I have now done quite a bit of fund-raising, and they told me that there were two top 'breast men' in London, one based at the Marsden, the other at the London Clinic, so I chose the London Clinic because it was nearer King's Cross station, and that was how I came to meet Tim Davidson.

And Breakthrough Cancer was absolutely right. He is a marvellous man about whom I cannot speak highly enough.

There were still decisions to be taken. Should I have a straightforward mastectomy, which only takes about an hour or so, or should I go for the full reconstruction surgery, which is altogether more complicated and is a ten-hour operation. Tim persuaded me to take the latter course of action, saying that I would regret it later if I did not. It was a tough decision to take because agreeing to a ten-hour procedure is a pretty traumatic ordeal, and things can go wrong.

Afterwards, I felt really weak, not helped by the fact that I also contracted MSSA, which is not to be confused with MRSA. MSSA is the one that reacts to penicillin, whereas MRSA is resistant to penicillin. I should make it clear that contracting MSSA had nothing to do with the London Clinic – there was no question of me having caught it because of a lack of cleanliness or anything like that. It is a condition that can occur naturally on your skin and when you have an open wound, you are more susceptible to being struck down by it.

The surgeon took muscle from my back to reconstruct my breasts, and I had to remain in hospital for two weeks after the operation, and then went home for a long recovery period. I had expected there to be pain in my chest, but it was actually my back that was the worst because there are so many nerve endings. It took me a good six weeks before I started to feel better, and during that period of rest and recuperation, my family were wonderful.

My first proper outing was a charity do for Prince Charles at Buckingham Palace, and as my strength returned I was able to take the dogs for long walks. Another side effect that I hadn't considered was that I was unable to use my right arm for a long time because the surgeon had removed all the lymph nodes.

Six months after the operation, Bill Kenwright asked me to take a leading role in *The Ideal Husband*. I had to learn the part in a week, which tends to focus the mind. But the role also required me to wear a low cut frock; this was something that I was extremely nervous about but I needn't have worried because everything was absolutely fine, and I am pretty sure that nobody would have guessed what I had been through. It was good enough to have been asked to play the part because it meant that I knew Bill had faith in my ability to pull it off, and it also did wonders for my confidence. I had been through what must surely be the most traumatic experience that any woman has to endure and I had come out the other side, fit and healthy and able to go back to work.

It set me fully on the road to recovery. Having breast cancer taught me to take nothing for granted, to live each day to the full. I now have yearly checks and, touch wood, everything is fine. In 2010 I had to have a new implant because they only last about ten years and the manufacturers are improving them all the time.

The wonderful thing about surgeons such as Tim Davidson is that they also do breast enlargements for women and it is thanks to the women who want bigger boobs that all these techniques have improved so dramatically. It is people such as myself who reap the benefits, so I say let's hear it for Katie Price please.

As a way of giving a little something back, I now do Breakthrough Cancer's annual moonwalk, which raises both money and awareness of breast cancer. In 2010, Sophie came along with me.

One of the most unfortunate aspects of my treatment was that I had to take a course of tablets called tamoxifen that hurtled me towards the menopause at breakneck speed. So not only did I have to come to terms with having had a full-blown mastectomy, but I also had to deal with all the symptoms of the Big M, such as sweats, having trouble sleeping, losing energy. And if I wasn't sweating then I was freezing. I had five years of that, and it was ghastly. But then I was able to stop taking the tablets and all of a sudden the symptoms all disappeared and I began to feel normal again. What a relief that was.

While I had been making *Collector's Lot* I met a man called Eric St John Foti who had a museum in a place called Downham Market that was devoted to Barbara Cartland, and he asked me if I had a few things that I had picked up throughout my career that would be suitable for a 'Liza Goddard corner'. The whole breast cancer episode and a sense of my own mortality were still very fresh in my mind and I thought to myself: "Well if I die, the children will probably just burn all my stuff." Instead, I thought that I might as well take it all round to Eric, but there was so much of it that the idea of a corner turned out to be an entire room devoted to me and my career.

In 2008, Eric's wife became ill and he was forced to sell up, but the man who bought it from him decided to keep the museum going and there remains a room in my name on the understanding that if my children ever decide that they want any of it they will able to collect it all. There are dozens of photographs, and memorabilia from various series that I did, including *Woof!* mugs.

The part that convinced me that I still had something to offer was in Alan Ayckbourn's *If I Were You*, which transformed my belief in myself. The role involves a depressed northern housewife who gradually turns into a man, and I knew that if I could carry that off, I could do pretty much anything I set my mind to.

Halfway through rehearsals I phoned David and told him I couldn't do it, and then I told Alan Ayckbourn I didn't think I could do it. His reaction? "Oh shut up Liza and just get on with it. Of course you can do it."

"Shut up and get on with it? What do you mean?"

But then I thought to myself that if Alan thought I could do it, then perhaps I really could. The funny thing is that with all parts you hit your head against a brick wall for a while and then suddenly there will be a eureka moment where you finally get what the character is all about. Slowly, but surely, you get the person inside of you – you have to somehow get them into your muscles, into your very being. You have to think their thoughts, and once I started thinking like a man, it became easier to act like a man and to walk like one. They even sit differently.

Once I 'got it' inside, it was a fantastic moment. This was a role like no other I had ever played and it truly transformed my thinking about what I was able to achieve as an actress. And to be able to do it after everything that I had been through was all the better.

I remember thinking to myself: "Liza, you have nothing to worry about. Here you are doing this amazing play, performing this incredibly challenging part in a fantastic theatre (the Stephen Joseph in Scarborough) for a genius. Life really doesn't get much better than this girl."

And the truth was that I would far rather have been doing that than anything else. This was a privilege and a pleasure. It was good for my soul, and a lot of my professional colleagues were jealous of me.

A lot of actor friends of mine who were coining it in doing TV work told me how lucky I was. I knew they were correct, but my reaction was still: "I am so lucky? You are the one making all the money."

I have always procrastinated, and that was one thing that didn't change after I recovered from the mastectomy. I don't know why it is but I put off learning my lines until the last possible moment, even though I know it is something that I have to do. I find it easier to go and ride my pony, walk the dogs or do the ironing. Anything, in fact, other than doing what I know I have got to do.

In the end I always get there – there is no choice because if you don't learn your lines then you don't work. And when I finally do buckle down to it, I am fairly well disciplined. It is easier when I am away from home because then I can focus, but when I am in Norfolk I am just hopeless.

I make sure that I look after myself now, and try to go to the gym two or three times a week. I also make my own aroma therapy oils, which is something that I really enjoy doing, and I also stay at a health farm on a fairly regular basis, which gives me a chance to relax and get all the knots ironed out of my body. And, of course, I walk the dogs and try to ride when I get the opportunity to do so.

CHAPTER 23
SYMPATHY PAINS

"Part of me thinks, even now, that David's condition was brought on by worrying about me. He is and always has been a worrier."

If I thought that all my troubles were behind me, I was about to be put straight. David and I were at home one night in 2001 when he realised that he had lost control of his bowel. There is no delicate way to put this – he had filled his pants. Worse than that, there was blood everywhere. I had spent all my life looking for the right man, and now I was thinking that I might be about to lose him – I am no nurse, but I didn't require any medical expertise to work out that this was bad news.

He was sent to the hospital for endless tests – waiting for the results of those was probably the most traumatic thing that I have ever had to endure. And you can imagine what poor David must have been going through. I felt that it had to be something serious but you keep your fingers crossed and you hope for the best, that maybe they will come back and tell you it was "just a virus. Go home, take these antibiotics and you will be fine in two weeks." That was never going to happen with David but the news was still pretty devastating when it came – he had bowel cancer.

I'd had my own experience with breast cancer but I had managed to come out the other side, and there is part of me that thinks, even now, that David's condition was brought on by worrying about me. He is and always has been a worrier.

The survival rate with bowel cancer is not high, and you would not wish the side-effects of chemotherapy on your worst enemy, but there were to be no quick fixes. David also had to go through an operation – nowadays it is done using keyhole surgery, but back then they opened him up. It was major surgery, but the doctors didn't get all the cancer that time, so the poor man had to go through a second operation.

While he was having all this treatment I was doing *Wild West* with Dawn French in Cornwall, so I was driving backwards and forwards from Cornwall to David's hospital bed in Norfolk and back again. It was exhausting and it was extremely traumatic, but the work kept me sane and gave me something to focus on other than the fact that I might be about to lose my husband.

Wild West was probably most remarkable for the start of Catherine Tate's television career really taking off. She had performed some minor roles in series such as *London's Burning* and *The Bill*, but her life really changed in 1996 when she decided to try her hand at stand-up comedy, and discovered that she had a gift for it. I can imagine nothing worse than walking out on stage to face a theatre full of people, all of them expecting me to make them laugh until their sides split. I would die on my feet, so I have nothing but admiration for people who can people if off, especially if they are women as I believe that for a woman to make it in stand-up, she has to be even better than the men.

After being spotted by Dawn French in Edinburgh, she gave Catherine a part in *Wild West*, and commented: "Catherine Tate is far too talented and must be destroyed." I also appeared in *Wild West*, so I saw Catherine's talent up close, and Dawn was right. Mind you, Dawn is also a comic genius – one of those people who can make you giggle just by pulling a face or raising an eyebrow.

Wild West had marvellous production values, and there was a lot of money behind it. The scripts were fantastic and it should have been a great success but the producers lost faith in it somehow and they didn't put the episodes out in the right order, so the episode that was intended to go out as the fifth was actually aired first. It meant that the continuity seemed to be all over the place, but if they had been shown in order there would have been no confusion.

It was gentle comedy and it should have been allowed to unfold gently.

As everybody knows, Dawn possesses talent in spades, but she was very much the boss, and things were done as she wanted them to be done. She is a very hard-working person, and I was quite surprised to find that, off stage, she was fairly quiet. I am sure that most people imagine that she is forever larking about and cracking jokes, and she can be very funny, but she is obviously a woman who, just like the rest of us, sometimes needs her own space.

She always appears to be larger than life when she appears on chat shows, but I can understand where that comes from. When you are invited on to a chat show it is usually because you have a new series, film, play or book to plug, and both the host and the audience have certain expectations.

I have done a fair number of chat shows in my time and I knew that what they wanted was Liza Goddard, the bubbly blonde actress with the somewhat fluffy, dizzy style, and I was happy to give them that. You develop a personality that is you but it is only a part of you and there are times when people expect you to do it, and you must never let them down. In real life you could not possibly be like that all the time because you would end up going insane, along with all the people with whom you share your life. It would be a nightmare.

It is like switching a light on and off. If people get the person they expect, and like what they see, there is a good chance that they will watch your series, film or play, or go out and buy your book.

Yes, it can be hard work going out and promoting your latest project, listening to the same questions over and over again, and having to give the same answers over and over again, but you always have to make the effort. You must treat each question as if it were the first time you had ever been asked it.

As for Catherine, she was very much from the same mould as Dawn – a brilliant comedy actress, but quiet off the set. In other words, completely normal. And she has gone on to do some wonderful work and create some fabulous comic characters.

Working with Dawn and Catherine was a marvellous tonic for me, and helped to keep me going through some pretty dark days. Having survived two lots of surgery, David then picked up clostridum difficile, one of those dreadful hospital superbugs, but he managed to come through that as well, and then he had six months of chemotherapy. Every Tuesday a nurse would come to the house and stick a needle in him. He didn't lose his hair, but his skin started peeling off, and he lost his sense of smell and taste – something he would never get back. It means that even now he will eat a meal and he doesn't know if it is good, bad or indifferent.

Sophie had had a daughter, Adelaide, when she was 18. In fact, her birth was one of the best moments of my life because I was there, and I was the first person to hold her.

Sophie and Adelaide came to live with us when the baby was one, and David was going through his treatment when she was about two years old. She would watch the nurse put the IV into David and would then toddle off and pretend to do the same thing to her dolly. One day they sent a student to the house to see to David and he could not find a vein; to my utter astonishment, Adelaide, who had been watching, said: "No, that is not how you do it. You do it like this..." And with that she demonstrated on her doll.

Having Adelaide around acted like a spur for David. She was a source of constant joy in his life. There were still no guarantees, of course, but then came the day of the tests when they told us that he was clear of the condition. David had taken on and beaten bowel cancer, helped along the way by a two-year-old little girl.

That wasn't really the end of the story, however. His battle to beat bowel cancer took a great deal out of him and he hasn't kept great health since. I suppose the most difficult thing for David is that he hasn't been able to work either. When you have had 18 inches of your bowel removed, your digestion is not the best, and that has been the case with him. He has also suffered heart problems, but he copes really well. He is very stoic – mind you, I believe that in such circumstances he would need to be. He just carries on, but that is what you have to do.

While David was recuperating I needed to carry on working but by then the television parts seemed to have dried up so I had no option but to take the theatre work that came along, and that meant being away from home for long periods of time, which was not something I would have chosen to do in those circumstances.

I have a lot to thank Bill Kenwright for – he kept me working, and helped to keep me from worrying endlessly about David's health. Not only that, but I got some great parts so it wasn't a case of slopping around in some dreadful play or other. I appeared in three Oscar Wilde plays, one by Alan Bennett, in which I starred with my dear friend Robert Powell.

Animal Aunts turned out to be a godsend during this period. I knew that David would not be well enough to look after all our dogs so I approached Animal Aunts for help – it is a firm that was set up by a woman called Jilly in Surrey, and I was one of her first customers. She was one of the first people in the country to house-sit for pets when the owners were away on holiday. In no time at all, the business had expanded and become really successful. They would send somebody along to feed and exercise the animals, and some of them almost became members of the family.

If you had as many dogs, chickens and horses as we had, it is far cheaper than putting them in kennels, and the added bonus is that the animals get to stay at home, so they don't get thrown out of their routine. I swear by them.

Sonia, whom I have already mentioned, looked after the animals, and even helped to nurse David back to health. She came to stay with us. One of the things he had to do was to drink plenty of water, and she took that on as one of her tasks, bringing him pints of water at various stages during the day and standing over him until he had drunk it.

She was an absolute rock, without whom I couldn't have achieved a fraction of what I did in the end. Tragically, she died of breast cancer, aged just 50.

Another was called Anna, who was a cousin of Catherine Zeta-Jones, the actress. It also helped that Sophie was living with us – she stayed with us from 2001 until 2005, when she met Steve, whom she then moved in with. I said to her: "You can't move out. You are taking my baby."

"No Mum, she's my baby actually."

"No she's not."

CHAPTER 24
MOVING ON

"While I am on the road, it is difficult for David. We talk all the time on the phone, but I am conscious of the fact that he would probably rather have me at home."

With Sophie gone and Thom married, we looked around at the house in Norfolk, with its barn and all its land and David and I came to the conclusion that it was too big for two of us. It also seemed to me that I was working flat out all the time just to keep the house. Apart from that, while I was away working, I wasn't comfortable with the thought of David rambling around in this big house. He was slowly getting better but we knew he would never fully recover.

I suppose he has come to terms with the fact that he has now reached an age when he is never going to feel better, when his body is letting him down. He can't do the things he used to do, such as going for long walks, which was something he always used to love doing. But no matter what has been thrown at him, he has never complained.

While I am on the road, it is difficult for David. We talk all the time on the phone, but I am conscious of the fact that he would probably rather have me at home. Fortunately, he has many interests in his life, not least the Hawk and Owl Trust's Sculthorpe Reserve, which he helped to set up.

A man called Nigel Middleton, who is the Hawk and Owl Trust's East Anglia Warden and Conservation Officer, was the inspiration behind the reserve. He spotted the land, rang David and told him that he had found what he was certain would be a perfect spot for a bird reserve. It was 37 acres of overgrown reedbeds, but Nigel and David mobilised an army of volunteers who transformed the land.

They got their reward with the return of the marsh harriers, which nest there every breeding season and feature on the wonderful BBC series *Springwatch*. We have also seen the return of other rare breeds of birds, along with the fungus, plants, otters, beetles and other insect life that form the eco-system that supports all this wildlife.

The trust now has 200 acres, and the entire project has been a huge success. I was president of the Hawk and Owl Trust for 20 years until 2010 when Chris Packham, the TV naturalist took over. I have also been involved with the Dogs Trust, the RSPCA, the Wildfowl and Wetlands Trust, the RSPB, the British Trust for Ornithology and International Animal Welfare.

In 2007 we sold the house and moved to a smaller one, still in Norfolk, and a bonus is the fact that we are just ten minutes away from Sophie and Adelaide. Sophie didn't want to be like me and spend most of her life working away from home. She wanted to do something that could be based from home. She was always very good at maths and we hoped that she would go to Cambridge University and get a degree in maths; instead, she ran away to have a baby. There isn't much to say about Adelaide's father other than the fact that it was a relationship that didn't work out, and I should know all about that.

Sophie is a graphic designer and decided to set up her own business. And very successful it is too. She developed a website called Eat Out Norfolk – the idea is that if you want, say, a vegetarian meal at a restaurant that allows dogs and children, you go to the website and key in your requirements and it will give you a list of the restaurants that will suit you. It is a simple idea, but all the best ideas are simple, and she is now looking into the possibility of expanding it to other parts of the country.

Every Wednesday morning she has a networking meeting, so Adelaide, my beloved grand-daughter, stays with David and I on Tuesday nights, and it is a sheer pleasure to have her.

I am immensely proud of both my children. Thom is married to Leanne and they have a son called Oscar. When Thom left university he did a journalism course in Birmingham and then went to work for a company called Network of the World, whose aim was to put television programmes on to computer. It was backed by a wealthy Chinese businessman but it was so far ahead of its time that it didn't work. Now, of course, you have the likes of iPlayer which does precisely the same thing. Sometimes, it is just all about timing and getting the lucky breaks at the right time.

At the time, people could not grasp the fact that you could watch TV programmes on a computer screen. Although it flopped, Thom came away with lots of skills and he ended up working children's television for the BBC. He loved it, but then the atmosphere at the Beeb changed and all of a sudden it wasn't such a great place to work. And then there was talk about people having to move to Manchester. He didn't want to move north, so used that as the excuse to leave and set up his own business, producing show reels.

A show reel pulls together all the clips from the television series and films that an actor might have been in, and showcases their talent. I suppose you could describe as a visual CV, but they are tightly edited, and seldom last longer than about three minutes. Even though I say so myself, they look and sound great, and everybody now needs one because they are such a good way of showing a potential casting director what an artist is capable of doing. They are also far more effective than a written CV.

He prepares them for everybody from drama students to Daniel Craig, the actor who plays James Bond. It may seem hard to believe that an actor of his stature needs a show-reel, but there will be some directors who know him only for playing 007, and will want to know what else he is capable of. There are some people who will say that he has done much better work than his part as James Bond – I'm not so sure about that. For my money, he doesn't strip down to his swimming trunks anything like often enough. The bottom line (ouch!) is that every actor needs a show-reel. Period.

Thom also has ideas of his own for a number of television series, and has been trying to get support and funding to turn those ideas into reality.

Having spent so much of their formative years sitting, bored out of their minds in a TV studio or by the side of a stage, both decided that they did not want to follow me into acting, and I can hardly blame them. I am delighted they both have 'proper' jobs in 'proper' professions.

I appeared on television a fair bit as the children were growing up, but they just accepted it as an everyday part of their lives. It was no big deal.

My mother continues to suffer with dementia and is now in a care home. I go and visit her and although I can never be certain what I am going to find, there are some priceless moments. She has a friend called Joyce at the home, and she is further down the road with dementia than my Mum and on one visit, Mum said: "Joyce, you remember Liza, don't you? She is my daughter."

Joyce replied: "I can't talk now. I am too busy talking to myself."

With that, she turned her back to us and carried on with her 'conversation'. I didn't know whether to laugh or cry, but I suppose the positive was that at least she knew she was doing it.

CHAPTER 25
A YEAR IN THE LIFE

"That's one of the things I love about you Liza. You are a proper actress, taking a part when you have no idea what it is yet," - Alan Ayckbourn

If you have a part in a soap or a regular TV drama it means that you know you have a good regular income coming in and, if you are very lucky, you might be able to indulge yourself by taking other parts during breaks in filming.

For those of us in the profession who don't have the luxury of a regular TV role, we have to take the work wherever and whenever we can. It becomes very difficult to say no to anything because it does cross your mind that eventually the phone will stop ringing and the roles will dry up completely.

I want to take you through a typical year in the life of Liza Goddard – a very busy year during which I worked almost without a break, but a year that I enjoyed tremendously.

As an actress, you have to make certain sacrifices – chief among those is that you seem to spend most of your life living away from home. There are mad dashes back to Norfolk on rare days off to make the most of your time with loved ones. It means that it is important that you get along with the people you work with because you end up living, eating, breathing and working with them.

The great thing about my profession is that it is full of like-minded people, and we have a tremendous amount of fun – without the laughs I think we may all go completely potty. Of course there is the occasional individual who puts your nose out of joint, but, thankfully, those people are few and far between.

In 2009 I finished touring *The Grass is Greener*, which turned out to be the last job done by Christopher Cazenove before his tragically premature death. He was a lovely man and it was a very happy show that also featured Sophie Ward and Jack Ellis. I finished *The Grass is Greener* on a Saturday and the following day I headed off to Bath, where I spent December 2009 and January 2010 doing a fabulous production of *Sleeping Beauty* written by Chris Harris, who starred as Nurse Nelly. The cast featured Gemma Bissix, who had appeared in *EastEnders* and *Hollyoaks* and who, in 2007, won the Villain of the Year award in the British Soap awards. I was the Good Fairy and Gemma was the Bad Fairy.

I love pantomime with a passion, and the best ones are those where the director also takes part. My very first was with the wonderful Lionel Blair, who directed and played Buttons. It is quite a common practice, and very often not only will they have directed it, but they also write it. The year before, I starred as Fairy Snowdrop in *Snow White and the Seven Dwarfs* in Norwich, which was wonderful because it meant that I could sleep in my own bed every night. Richard Gauntlett, who is a brilliant comedian, wrote that script and played the dame too. He also directed the show.

If you have the director on stage with you every night, the show remains fresh and real. Richard is a pantomime buff, a real enthusiast, and he writes wonderful scripts and is a tremendous dame.

Although Gemma had appeared in two of the country's biggest TV soaps, appearing in front of millions of viewers, she hadn't done much theatre work, and it can be pretty daunting if you are not used to it. Chris was wonderful with her, and she quickly grew into the part. From the outset she had made it clear that she wanted to do things properly – she didn't want to just be seen as a '*Hollyoaks* name'. To watch her grow into the part was tremendous.

The thing with panto is that the goody and the baddie both have to be believable – Lionel Blair taught me that, and he was absolutely correct. If people don't want to boo and hiss whenever the baddie appears on stage, then your panto is doomed to fail. The children in the audience believe every word, so the only person who can come out of character and talk to them with a few asides is the dame, or Buttons.

We started the pantomime in Bath in December and it ran through until almost the end of January. We had some bitterly cold weather, during which the boiler in the digs in which I was staying decided to pack up – strangely enough, precisely the same thing happened to us later in the year in Scarborough, and we ended up with no hot water. At one point, the only place we could wash and shower was at the theatre.

During the worst of the weather in Bath, I had five days without heating or hot water. It was awful – so bad, in fact, that I went to bed each night fully clothed. Luckily, when you are doing pantomime you get up early in the morning, have breakfast and then you go to the theatre, where you remain until 10pm. The only exceptions to this rule are Christmas Day, when you get a day off, and New Year's Day.

It was nice and warm in the theatre, so it was no hardship to be there for 12 hours a day. It is normal to do two shows a day, sometimes three, and you have to fit your meals around that. It is hard work, but it is also very rewarding – there is nothing like the feeling you experience when you look out into the auditorium and see row upon row of children loving every minute of the show that you are putting on for them.

It is also very rewarding from a financial point of view – panto is well-paid, which I guess is just one of the reasons why so many well-known actors and actresses sign up for it. I often wonder what the Americans make of it all though – they have nothing like panto in the United States, so what goes through the mind of somebody like Pamela Anderson when she arrives at the theatre and is given the script to read for the first time?

I am pretty sure that she was totally bewildered by it all. Oh yes she was!

It is a wrench to be away from your family, of course it is, but it comes with the territory. It is fine when you are on stage because you get lost in the part you are playing, and the adrenalin pumps through your body when you are getting the laughs in the right places, and when the audience participates.

When we finished at 10pm, the younger members of the cast would head off into the night and party into the small hours, but I couldn't imagine anything worse at my age. For me, going out just wasn't an option, so I would head back to my digs, have something to eat, watch a bit of television and then go to bed – otherwise I simply wouldn't have had the energy to work.

Christopher Biggins is one of the greatest party people I have ever met, but even he lives like a monk during pantomime season.

Remember that we are talking about a role that involves singing and dancing, acting and flying. Okay, so we don't exactly fly, but we do hang in the air in a trapeze-like contraption that sends us whizzing through the air, and it is very tiring.

Between shows, I would put on my dressing gown, have a ready meal, watch *Come Dine With Me*, have a nap and then get ready for the evening show. Those short sleeps have become a very important part of my routine, and they really do work. If you can get into the habit of closing your eyes and dozing off for anything up to an hour, you will be amazed at how good and how refreshed you feel when you waken up. I swear by it, as do most of my colleagues. It is a great way to recharge your batteries.

I hate leaving my home, but I always end up having a good time when I am away because the people I work with are such good fun. Obviously it helps that we are like-minded individuals. Even my 10-year-old grand-daughter turned round recently and said to me: "I love actors – they are such fun." Very perceptive for one so young.

After finishing the panto, I was home for February but had to do the photo shoot for the posters to advertise Alan Ayckbourn's *Communicating Doors* in Scarborough – that involved driving all the way from Norfolk to Yorkshire and back in the same day. I also had March and most of April at home, and then went to London to begin rehearsals for a production of *If I Were You*, again by Ayckbourn. I had premiered it in 2005 with Jack Ellis and Ayden Callaghan.

During that time I also took the opportunity to take part with my daughter Sophie in the Moon Walk, which saw us walking more than 13 miles through the night to help raise money for breast cancer research. When I did the first Moon Walk, 600 people took part, but this time there were 15,000 in Hyde Park. It was a great experience.

We then took the play on a four-week tour that took in Windsor,

Richmond, Blackpool, Eastbourne and Cambridge. It was very much a case of: "If it's Wednesday, it must be Eastbourne." It is a bit like a circus. After one week in a given town or city, we all up sticks and move on to the next venue.

I had found out in October 2009 that I would be doing the two Ayckbourn plays in Scarborough. He offered me a part in *Communicating Doors* and asked if I would also like to appear in *Life of Riley*. I immediately said yes.

"That's one of the things I love about you Liza. You are a proper actress, taking a part when you have no idea what it is yet," he said. And it is true, I didn't know because he hadn't actually written it at that point.

If I Were You finished on June 26 and I had a week off before heading to Scarborough, but not before something incredible happened on June 27 – Thom's son, Oscar, was born. So now I had a grandson, the most beautiful little boy. On the same day I had already agreed to go to Soham to hand out awards for a wonderful organisation called Viva, of which I am vice-president. It is run by an extraordinary man called Dan Schumann and is a children's drama group. No child is turned away, and they put on some wonderful musicals. They have won awards at the Edinburgh Festival, and their only source of funding is a shop in Soham. Each year they have an awards ceremony which ends with the kids putting on a show for everybody.

These are just ordinary children who have a passion for entertaining. One or two of the kids have gone on to attend drama school, but that is not really what Viva is about – it is there to give them confidence, and it wouldn't exist if it were not for Dan. Surprisingly, there are a lot of boys in the company, and they put on a production of *Les Miserables* in Cambridge which was absolutely tremendous.

185

Before heading to Scarborough, I attended the party to celebrate John Nettles' retirement from *Midsomer Murders*, and that was a fantastic opportunity to catch up with an actor who has become a very dear friend. I also saw lots of other people that I hadn't seen for years. It was a great party, as you can imagine. He did 80 episodes of *Midsomer Murders*, and I had a brief cameo appearance in one of them. It was such a lovely show to do and, once again, a great cast of characters who obviously got along famously with one another.

Ironically, Laura Howard, who played his daughter, Cully, appeared with me in *Communicating Doors* and *Life of Riley*.

On Monday, 5 July, we had something called a 'meet and greet' at the Stephen Joseph Theatre where everybody involved in the production came along, so I got to meet Frank the carpenter, Michael the painter, the ushers, all the front-of-house staff. Everybody stands up and introduces themselves – it is a great idea, and the point of it is to emphasise that everybody is a member of a team. It can be quite an alarming process if you have never done it before; fortunately, I had.

For many years, Alan Ayckbourn was artistic director at the theatre, but that role is now filled by Chris Monks, who is the steadying hand at the tiller.

Having introduced ourselves to one another, the entire company then poured into the rehearsal room, where everybody listened to the first read through of *Communicating Doors*, the first of the two plays we were putting on. Even now, after all the years I have spent in the business, I still found that a terrifying prospect. I had read the play but this was the first time that I had to read my lines out loud, in front of a room full of comparative strangers. Again though, it succeeds in helping us all to form a unique bond, and it is a very clever process.

The following day we were straight into full rehearsals. When Alan addressed the cast, everybody made copious notes of everything that he said – they always do. It is part and parcel of working for him because he always says the right thing at the right time, and he knows exactly how he wants each part to be played.

Right at the beginning, Alan gave everybody a complete schedule for the entire process. So, for example, on the first Tuesday I knew that I would be required at 2pm and we would be going from pages 20 to 30. Page 20 was my first scene – in the morning they had gone from page one through to page 19. It is all planned military precision. On Wednesday it was pages 30 to 43 in the morning, and then a recap in the afternoon.

He is unique in so many ways. Most directors have the entire cast sitting around together, whether they are needed or not. He has never done that, so you would only be called by Alan for your bit.

The beauty of this system is that you know what you have to learn, and you know when you have to learn it, and it makes everything so much easier. Monday, pages 68 through to 74 – that's what you had to learn, and that is what you learnt. If there was a day when they were going through a sequence of pages that did not involve my character then I would be given the day off. When you think about it, it makes perfect sense. Why on earth would a director want you hanging around the theatre if you were not required?

I should tell you that there are no tricks to learning lines, well not for me at any rate. For me, it is all about reading the lines over and over again until they finally sink in. I know that there are some actors who used various trigger words and phrases to memorise their lines, but that has never worked for me.

A normal rehearsal day would begin at 10.30am, with a break for coffee at 11.30am when Alan would usually deliver some killer anecdotes, or Alandotes as we called them. The thing with these stories is that they are all pertinent to the show. He doesn't like to waste words, even when he is speaking them. So we laughed a lot and then got back to work, stopping for lunch at 1pm, and then back to work at 2pm through until 5.30pm if you were not working in the evening. There would be another coffee break, usually at 3.30pm. I had been told about the anecdotes by an actress friend called Elizabeth Bell who had worked with Alan is the past, so I thought I knew what to expect.

She was in the Ayckbourn company at the National Theatre when he directed *View from the Bridge*, which Arthur Miller said was the best version of that play he had ever seen. Elizabeth also appeared in *Family Business*, and people didn't believe it was the same actress because the parts were so completely different and she pulled them off so wonderfully well.

Elizabeth grew up in Scarborough and saw her first Ayckbourn play when she was 14 years old, and worked with him in Stoke on Trent. She said to me: "Listen to everything he says." And as I bumped in to other people who had worked with him, they all said the same thing.

The baton has now passed to me, and I will tell actors and actresses who haven't worked with him before to look, listen and learn. Nothing that he says is just to get cheap laughs; it is always about the play, about the way he wants it done.

With Alan it is always intense periods of work, followed by tea and cake and chat, and then he would expect every member of his cast to go away and do their work. By that, I mean that you go back to your digs and learn your lines and take on board any and all directions he may have given you.

It helped me that I was sharing accommodation with the other two girls who were in *Communicating Doors* (Laura Doddington and Laura Howard) because we could learn our lines together in the evening. We would also correct each other until we knew that we were all word perfect. With both girls being called Laura, we decided it would be easier to give them nicknames, but they both decided that they wanted to be called Lolly, so that was no help at all. The three of us used to come home at night, put gunge in our hair and then apply a face-mask before sitting down in front of the TV and laughing endlessly.

From the second week on, Alan wanted us to be rehearsing without holding a copy of the script. The funny thing is that you know the lines when you are sitting in front of the mirror in the morning, you know them when you are lying in the bath, and you know them when you are walking through the town on the way to the theatre, but then you stand up in the rehearsal room and your mind goes blank and you can't remember a single word.

"But I knew this an hour ago, so how come I don't know it now?"

We also work at weekends, of course. It is intensive, but that is the only way. All of this happens in a rehearsal room until, eventually, the time comes when Alan wants us to go out on stage and do it, complete with all the props. My big scene in *Communicating Doors* involved me being thrown over a balcony every night (as you do), so that was something else I had to learn. And then there was the fight sequence that had to be learnt in such a way that ensured nobody ever got hurt.

There is a huge difference between sitting around in a rehearsal room saying the words, and then going out on stage and doing it as if it were for real, but that is the point at which the play comes to life.

After a month of rehearsals, *Communicating Doors* opened on 5 August, 2010, and three days later we kicked off the whole process again by starting rehearsals for *Life of Riley*, which was Alan's 74th play – so we were all rehearsing during the day and then going on stage in the evening and performing *Communicating Doors*. On top of that, Alan had obviously watched the evening performances and given us all notes of things that we had to change, so not only were we having to learn a new script, but we were having to put things right with the other one. The only difference to the procedure was that once *Communicating Doors* had opened to the public, our rehearsals during the day would end at about 4pm in order to give us time to unwind and prepare for the evening performance.

It may sound difficult, but my brain loves that type of a challenge, and I just got stuck in and did what had to be done. I don't mind admitting that I was exhausted at times, all the more so because *Communicating Doors* is quite a physical play, one that takes a great deal out of you because there is a lot of running around, and that is without taking into account the fight scene and being thrown over a balcony. Thank goodness I am pretty fit.

The audience also tend to get involved. There is a line in *Communicating Doors*: "If I don't go to bed soon, I shall die..." And when it is said, the audience almost always respond with: "Oooooh no," because they just know that something awful is going to happen.

One thing I have found is that when I am working like this it is impossible to read a book. Even a cereal packet is dangerous because I find myself looking at the ingredients and starting to memorise them, exactly as I would if I were learning a script. I can't pass a road sign or any form of advertising without starting to memorise it all. I guess it is because my brain is in a state of high alert because I have learnt one script and now I am learning another.

Real life disappears out the window at times like that. I find that I cannot even watch the TV, listen to the news or read a newspaper, for fear that I would stand up on stage that night and start spouting forth with the entire contents of that day's Daily Mail. We would get every Sunday off so I would jump into the car and drive home, and then spend all day Sunday learning my lines before having to get back into the car on the Monday morning and setting off for Yorkshire again.

And then there are all the little idiosyncrasies about theatre life – in Scarborough, we had the 'mugs of shame'. Everybody is allocated their own mug, upon which they put their name, initials or distinctive mark. The only unwritten rule is that when you have finished your tea or coffee, you must wash your mug and put if back where you found it. It is considered extremely bad form to leave it lying around for somebody else to clean. Inevitably, there will be the odd person who forgets to clean their mug and leaves it on a chair or a table. Those cups are removed and installed in the 'mugs of shame' gallery, and if the owner still doesn't get what it is all about and leaves his or mug out again, it will be locked away in a cupboard, forcing them to ask for it to be returned – and that is regarded as the ultimate humiliation!

When you spend so much time away from home you have no option but to lead an alternative life. My car needed a service – if I had been at home in Norfolk I would know who to take it to; instead, I had to make some inquiries and found a reliable garage in York. And, of course, I had to find a hairdresser because the salon I used back at home does not open on a Sunday. I was lucky to find a great branch of Tony and Guy in York. The character I played in Communicating Doors was somebody who took great pride in her appearance, so I also had to locate a good manicurist. I spent a lot of time in that play in my bare feet so, yes, I also need a pedicurist. It is not easy being an actress you know! Oh yes, and then there was day I went into Bettys tearoom in York, had a Florentine and lost a chunk of my tooth, so then I also had to locate a dentist. That was a day when I had to fly by the seat of my pants because the dentist gave me an injection, my mouth swelled up and I couldn't talk. Under normal circumstances, that wouldn't be a problem, but I was due on stage that night. Fortunately, the swelling went down in time for the show.

I should say that when I go home and have, say, a month off, I find it incredibly easy to switch off. I have a pony and I love riding – it is one of the best ways I know of unwinding and losing yourself in your own thoughts. I also have a grand-daughter whom I adore and love spending time with. And then, when it is time to go back to work, I find it is quite easy to switch back on again. You do what you have to do.

Anyway, on 13 September, we started doing the technical runs for Life of Riley with all the props and furniture in place, and a few days later we opened and, suddenly, we were no longer rehearsing during the day and it was really strange. Alan got very emotional just before we opened Life of Riley.

He usually gives a marvellous speech to the cast and crew at the end of rehearsals., and this was to be no exception:

"Right, you are going live in front of an audience and you will find that they laugh and you will be grateful and then after a time you start demanding laughs with menaces. 'Come on you buggers, laugh.' You have to try and hang on to that first feeling when you didn't know they were going to laugh because you didn't know you were funny. Five weeks ago we started at rehearsals with 12 people – six actors and six characters and over the weeks the actors have taken over the characters and made them real, made them their own. Now my baby is going out of my control, into the audience, and now it belongs to you. It is no longer mine."

That is the way he must have felt for every play he wrote. He would come and watch us, and of course he passed on some notes, but he truly feels that when he gives one of his plays to a group of actors it is no longer his. I should stress that the notes he passes to the actors are not a list of complaints – he simply passes on his thoughts and wishes as to things that could be done to make a performance even better, and he will always give credit where it's due.

"That's very good, and that was excellent so keep that, but maybe we could get rid of this and try that instead."

It was a huge honour to be one of the cast that took *Life of Riley* on to a stage for the first time – nobody had seen it before. We had all read it and we knew that it was a great piece of writing, but until we walked on to that stage and delivered it for the first time, we had no idea whatsoever how the audience would react. Obviously, any fears that we might have had were unfounded because they loved it.

No matter how long you have been in this business, you never get over first-night nerves. I suffer as badly now as I have always done, and I am glad that I do because it proves that I care about what I am doing. There have been times when I have stood in the wings with heart pounding so hard and so fast that I have been convinced all the audience could see my blouse moving in and out. Once I get on stage and get into character they go, but before that I feel sick to the pit of my stomach. I think that I must be an adrenalin junkie.

I am often asked how it is possible to perform the same part and repeat the same lines day after day while still keeping it fresh. I am sure that every actor has his or her own way of doing it, but I go on stage each night with the thought in my mind that I am doing the play for the very first night. As I said earlier, different audiences react in different ways, and that helps too.

There are some plays when I have found myself thinking: "I can't bear to say these lines again." Thankfully, those are few and far between, and it never happens with an Alan Ayckbourn play, mostly because his characters have such a rich inner life. I find something new about the character almost every time I walk on stage. It also helps to know that the audience are on your side from the second you appear; they have paid for their tickets and they are willing you to be good. They want to feel that they have had their money's worth and that they have been entertained, so you feel a duty to provide them with that entertainment. There are few things more rewarding than hearing an audience laugh, or to be aware that, at the most poignant moment in a story, members of the audience are crying because the story being played out in front of them has moved them to tears.

As a performer, I love it if we have a man or a woman in the audience with a distinctive laugh because that person will set everybody else off. It is not always perfect of course, and there are nights where you step out on stage and give the same performance that you gave the night before, and the night before that, and yet you get the sense that the audience is not with you, and they don't laugh at the lines that had last night's crowd in hysterics. I can't explain it, I really can't.

I heard a great line on the radio: "People will applaud out of politeness, but they will not laugh out of politeness." And how very true that is. Alan takes a novel view on this. "Well they could be Norwegian," he says. Yes, they could be, but you can't always rely on that. Perhaps they just think you are awful.

I remember rehearsing one of Alan's plays and asking him: "Alan, why have you called this play a comedy? It is brilliant, but it is not a comedy. It is not at all funny."

He just looked at me as if I were stupid. We carried on rehearsing and then out we went for opening night and, of course, the audience were in hysterics. And that is why I act and he writes. He also has this gift for being able to write brilliant stories that get a message over despite the comedy or maybe because of it. You always know where you are going with his work because it is structured – there is a beginning, a middle and an end. Alan's work always has a resolution. Each act has a beginning, a middle and an end, but he also has the gift for being able to set up a gag in the opening act, something that the audience tuck away in the back of their minds, and then he will deliver the payoff in the final act. The audience remember throwaway lines.

Particularly in the round, you have to focus absolutely on what you are doing and try to be as real as possible. Comedy is also the most difficult thing to pull off because it is all about timing, and I am certain that is one of the reasons why Alan is so fastidious, and so determined that his cast get it right, and get it right from the very start. You also have to listen out for the laughs and when they come you have to pause for a second so that the audience don't miss the next line. It is extremely difficult to get it right every time.

If the actor standing in front of you has a really funny line, you have to learn to feed them; the better you can do that, the better the laugh he or she will get. I spent 15 months in the West End doing *No Sex Please,*

We're British, with David Jason, and I learnt a huge amount about comic timing during that run. This was long, long before Del Boy came along to change his life forever, but even then it was clear that David was a genius when it came to comedy acting – not only that, but he was a thoroughly decent man too. It is a rare combination.

While I was in Scarborough, David suffered a major health scare. We thought that his bowel cancer had returned, and it was a dreadfully worrying time. He had to go to hospital for tests on 13 October, 2010, and because they had decided not to knock him out, it meant that he would get to know at the same time as the hospital staff whether or not the news was bad. I longed to be with him but we don't have understudies in rep, which meant it really was a case of "the show must go on'.

His appointment was for 5.30pm, and I ended up going on stage that night not knowing what the outcome was. I don't quite know how I got through it. David was in my mind constantly. Eventually I got to speak to him after the performance. He had been given the all clear. All of you who have been through a similar experience will know the sense of relief and gratitude I felt at that moment. It was like a huge weight had been lifted from my shoulders.

There was one night in September while we were in Scarborough when Laura Howard had to go home because it looked like her father was going to die (sadly, he did pass away). Ruth Gibson, a great friend and fellow actress who had come to Yorkshire to see the show as a member of the audience was told: "Ruth, you are on." It was an actor's nightmare.

But Ruth performed heroically. Alan Ayckbourn took her through her lines in the afternoon and gave her directions and acting notes. Fortunately, that evening we were putting on *Communicating Doors* and

Ruth's part was not as detailed as it would have been had she been forced to step in the breach for *Life of Riley*, but this was still a daunting prospect for any performer.

Before she went on stage she asked: "What do you want me to wear?"

"Bra and pants, Ruth."

"Bra and pants? You are joking."

But they were not joking – the part called for her to come on stage in her underwear. She had been training for the Berlin Marathon, so she was in great shape.

Ruth said: "I am in a win-win situation here anyway because if I make a mistake the audience will make allowances for me because they know I am standing in for Laura."

For the rest of us it was absolutely terrifying because we had to be spot on in order to make things as easy as possible for Ruth. Because she hadn't had the time to read the entire play, she didn't know when to come on stage – fortunately, in her first three scenes she was due to come on with another actor, so she was able to take her cue from him. But there was one scene where she had to come on to the stage on her own, and she later told me that she was standing there thinking: "I have no idea when I am due to go on." One of the complications was that the only part of the script she had been given was with her lines.

She produced a flawless performance, and before she left she told me that she was never coming to see me in another play. She then drove home to London on the Friday, caught a flight to Berlin on the Saturday and ran the Berlin Marathon on the Sunday in four hours and 20 minutes. Now that is what I call a trouper. Absolutely magnificent.

You will remember that I told you about the 'mugs of shame'. Ruth featured in a memorable mug story. She went to make herself a cup of coffee and her cup had vanished. She insisted that she hadn't left it out and, sure enough, it was nowhere to be found. We had no joy in the 'mugs of shame' and it wasn't in the cupboard either. But then ransom notes started to appear: 'We will return your mug unharmed but only if you give us a large packet of Maltesers'.

Various members of the cast sent her assorted ransom notes, and had a ball doing so, but Ruth never did find her mug. Perhaps it really was kidnapped. One of the things I most enjoy about my profession is that almost everybody possesses a sense of fun, but we will all rally round if somebody needs our help and support.

Many things have changed. In the 'old days' theatres were either subsidised or funded by the government, but that is no longer the case. Lottery funding will go towards buildings, but not people or day-to-day running costs. So if a theatre can sell out a play for a month or two, such as the Stephen Joseph Theatre did when we were appearing in the Ayckbourn plays, then it will raise enough money to keep it going. In the main, actors are not stupid people – we accept that we are not going to earn huge sums of money in towns such as Scarborough, but we do earn a good living and, as an added bonus, we play a small part in keeping local theatre alive, which is vital for all of us.

And that is a point worth stressing – the theatre is for everybody. There are still some people who say: "Oh, it's not for the likes of us." But that simply isn't true. I would also like to see more young people coming to the theatre – audiences are predominantly middle-aged or elderly. I guess that is because those are the generations with the most disposable income to hand, but we need to find a way to get younger people in because they represent the future. Youth theatre is a step in the right direction, and many theatres go out of their way to open their doors to schoolchildren, but it is clear that more needs to be done. Perhaps we as actors should get out there on a more regular basis, climb up onto our soap boxes and spread the word more vigorously than we do at present.

While I was in Scarborough, I was asked to attend a women's charity dinner in the town but then realised that they also wanted me to make a speech of some sort, so I stood up in front of them and said: "Good afternoon ladies, thank you for inviting me. I was a bit worried when I realised that you wanted me to get up and talk to you because there really are not many subjects that I know a great deal about. Anyway, I put my thinking cap on and suddenly the idea came to me. I know a lot about mucking out horses and ponies, so that is going to be the subject of my talk to you."

It was one of those moments where I wished I had taken a camera with me – their faces were a picture.

"Then I had another thought. I am involved with the Hawk and Owl Trust and I know a lot about vultures, so I thought that I might give you the vulture lecture..."

There was that look again...

"No? Okay, I will talk about me instead..." And I did, and it seemed to go down pretty well.

On Tuesday, 12 October, something most peculiar happened. I had been to York during the day to get my hair done, and then I drove to Scarborough, had something to eat, had a one-hour nap and arrived at the theatre, full of beans and ready to get on stage. We were putting on a performance of *Life of Riley*, and it was a sell-out. Well at least I thought we were putting on a performance of *Life of Riley*, but when I got to the theatre I was told that there was a serious problem with the stage lift – it sits under the main stage and goes down about 60 feet to the workshop area. This thing is so good that you can perform one play in the afternoon and a totally different one in the evening, with the lift being used to move all the props and furniture. It saves a huge amount of time, and allows the crew to do a complete turnaround in about 30 minutes. Trust me, that is quick.

There had been a problem a couple of days earlier and the crew had to order a new part from Germany, where the lift was made. Everything seemed to be fine. Because it was German, you won't be surprised to learn that it was normally very reliable but then it broke down with our set 30 feet below the level of the stage and no matter what they tried, they could not get it to work, so they had to cancel the show, something that had never happened to me before. I was once only able to do half a show – I was appearing in a matinee in Hull, and we managed to get through the first half without any difficulty. When we got to the interval, the big iron safety curtain came down, but they were unable to raise it again, so the second half had to be scrapped. We all thought that we would get the evening off until we were told that the only person in the entire country who could repair the curtain just so happened to be in Hull on that very day. The best laid plans...

The worst thing about the incident in Scarborough was that we were unable to let the audience know, so 400 people turned up at the Stephen Joseph Theatre on the night of 12 October expecting to see a performance of *Life of Riley*, only to be told it had been cancelled. In the end, we put on an extra matinee on the Friday and the front of house staff frantically tried to get in touch with everybody who had been so disappointed on the Tuesday. Obviously, a high percentage of those people were at work, but at least we managed to put on a show for some of them.

We also had to do a matinee on the Thursday and on the Saturday, which meant doing six performances in three days. The Saturday marked the end of the stint in Scarborough, which was probably just as well because we were all knackered. But there was very little time to draw breath because we then we had to take the plays on the road for a further five weeks, starting off in Stoke-on-Trent, where we did not have any matinees to do and that gave us the opportunity to get out and about during the day and see a bit of the surrounding area. I am a member of the National Trust because no matter where you are in the country there is almost always a National Trust property within striking distance.

Being away from home can be difficult, but one of the joys is that it does afford you the opportunity to visit various places and make the most of any time you get off during the day. A lot of actors play golf, with the job giving them the opportunity to play just about every day if they so wish.

You may wonder how we find good digs when we are touring. The trick is to ask other actors for their recommendations. I find that word of mouth is always the best way. The minute I get the dates and venues for a play, I start ringing round to get my digs organised.

We spent three weeks at the Victoria Theatre in Stoke on Trent and because it was only a two-and-a-half hour drive back home, I would head back to Norfolk after we had finished work on a Saturday, and drive back to Stoke on the Monday. After that we went off to the Old Laundry Theatre in Bowness on Windermere, on the banks of Lake Windermere, where we stayed in a timber-clad lodge – what a beautiful part of the world but unfortunately it was just too far from home to consider driving back.

The Old Laundry is a tiny theatre, with seating for 120 people, built by a designer called Roger Glossop, who has done quite a bit of work with Alan. He was also involved in setting up the Beatrix Potter Experience, which is based in the theatre building. Matinees were quite an experience because we would be performing on one side of the wall, and you would have the Beatrix Potter Experience unfolding on the other side. Because it is such a small, intimate theatre, it is a bit like having a conversation with the audience, and I absolutely loved it.

I dragged the entire crew along to the pencil museum in the Lake District, and although they originally didn't want to go, I have to tell you that learning how a pencil was made was fascinating. Think about the work that goes into it – the graphite has to be mined, then you have to get precisely the right sort of cedarwood and then there is the whole process of turning the graphite into a thin strip and inserting it into the wood.

During the Second World War everybody was issued with grey pencils because there was a shortage of paint, but the air force were given green ones, and inside each would be a compass and a map of Germany – the idea was that if they were ever shot down, they would be able to find their way home. It was invented by the man on whom they based Q, from the James Bond books and films.

I was in the Lake District for two weeks and so, finally, at the end of November, I was able to get back home, just in time for the worst snow we had experienced in years.

No sooner was I back home than I had to get back in the car and drive to the north-west of England, where I did a charity gig with my dear friend Robert Powell at Manchester Grammar School.

And then, towards the end of January 2011, after eight weeks at home, the whole thing started all over again and we took *Life of Riley* to

Guildford in Surrey. Although the cast obviously knew the lines, we had to rehearse the plays all over again because the theatre in Guildford has a proscenium stage, and we had been used to performing them in the round.

I get asked sometimes if I feel that I am on a treadmill, and I suppose that if I didn't enjoy my work to much then I might have to say yes. When I have been home for a while it is much more difficult to get in the car and the road for a new venue, but it never takes me long to get back into my stride, mainly because I get to work with so many wonderful people.

Bringing a freshness to the same part every day is what my job is all about, and I was no longer able to do that then it would be time to call it a day. You have to go out on stage and try to imagine that every performance is the first one, and you also have to listen to your fellow performer's lines and treat them as if it were the first time you had ever heard them. It also helps when you are doing a top quality play because sometimes you hear a line and, like a bolt from the blue, you suddenly get what the writer was trying to convey, even though you might have heard the line every night for a month or more. You will be surprised by how much you can get from just listening – and that applies to everyday life too.

I enjoy touring, especially if we are only staying in each place for a week. I wish that I could tell you that all the plays I have toured with have been classics, but I suspect that some of you might well have seen one or two pieces I have done that I would really rather forget.

There have been some stinkers, most notably *Murder by Misadventure* which I did with Robert Powell. We had to tour with it, and the script was awful and everybody knew that it was awful. But it paid the bills. On the other hand, we had a great time while we were doing it. We also toured Alan Bennett's *Single Spies*, which was a great play that was incredibly rewarding to do, and which received great acclaim.

Robert is an actor I regard as a close friend. He is married to Babs, who used to dance with Pan's People on Top of the Pops, and got married when I was expecting Thom.

We like to do the same things, so we would meet up in the morning after breakfast, get hold of a map, unfold it on the table in front of us and decide where we wanted to go for the day.

As well as the map, you must also have a copy of the good beer guide because if a country pub sells good beer, you can be certain that it will also sell top-notch food. We would then plan a route that would take us to somewhere where we could have a nice walk in the country, then go to the pub for lunch, go for another walk and finish it off with a drive back, leaving time to have a bit of a rest before going on stage in the evening. Sometimes you can even fit in a visit to a stately home as well. That is my idea of the perfect touring day, and Robert enjoys it too.

When you are on tour, you usually arrive on a Monday, Tuesday is normally the day when you meet the press, and there would probably be a matinee on a Wednesday, which would leave Thursday and Friday clear to do something like this.

We have been very lucky, and have never broken down or managed to get ourselves lost. There was one occasion when we were working in Blackpool and Robert said: "You know Liza, we could head off to the Lake District and do a lot of the lakes in a day."

It is one my favourite parts of the country so I readily agreed and off we went, with me at the wheel of my new car, which had an automatic gearbox. Robert was in the passenger seat reading the manual and said:

"Do you know if you flick this switch on top of the gear lever it will take you down the gears?"

"No, I didn't know that, but it sounds useful."

Robert was navigating and was confident that we could fit in ten lakes, which seemed rather a lot to me. Sure enough, we managed to do it, visiting places such as Grassmere and Keswick, but we had to come back by climbing to the top of the treacherous Hardnott Pass. It was early November and there was no turning back if we wanted to get back to Blackpool in time for the evening show. As we approached the pass there was a low-loader coming in the opposite direction and on the trailer was the remains of a car that had clearly been in a frightful accident. Robert said: "I bet that fell off the road."

Sure enough, as we hit the road going into the pass I realised that the surface was covered in ice, even though it had been gritted. I was terrified and the thought occurred to me that we, too, might slide off the road, tumble down the hill and die. Luckily, because Robert had read the manual, we were able to drop down the gearbox and we carefully negotiated the slope. I remember Robert saying: "Liza, look at the views. They are magnificent."

"Views? Are you mad? We are going to die!"

But of course we didn't die, although when we got to the top we both looked at one another and took a deep breath because now we had to go down the other side of the hill. Fortunately, there was nothing coming the other way and we eventually got to the bottom, where I had to stop the car because I was shaking so much through sheer blind terror.

We arrived back in Blackpool at 6.30pm – and were back on stage one hour later as if nothing had ever happened. But what an incredible day we'd had. A terrific adventure.

Robert and I regularly do recitations together for a chap called Clive Conway, who is a brilliant flautist. It is essentially an evening's entertainment during which Robert and I recite poetry and do bits of Shakespeare, mixed in with bits of amusing dialogue, and then Clive plays the flute and Christine Croshaw plays piano. It is an absolute delight because we visit some of the country's 1,500 small theatres that each hold 100-200 people, so it means you are guaranteed an intimate atmosphere. In many ways it is rather quaint and old-fashioned but it is no less enjoyable for all that. People love it because we take them through every emotion.

I also used to do them with John Mortimer, who was one of the great raconteurs. He lived an amazing life, something that hit me right between the eyeballs one night when he was talking about the Oz trial. When he worked as a barrister he seemed to have great fun all the time, and it was the same with his work as a dramatic author and screenwriter. He seemed to enjoy everything he did. What a talent.

He said: "I much preferred murderers as clients Liza. People who are getting divorced will ring you up at two in the morning to tell you that their partner has taken the dog, or the TV or whatever. Murderers, on the whole, can't get to the phone so they never disturb your sleep. And of course the other thing with most murderers is that once they have killed the one person in their life who was really bugging them they become completely calm and will never commit another crime. Divorce cases just go on and on and on." He was a great wit and it was always a joy to spend time in his company.

Clive doesn't just use actors – he also get the likes of Ann Widdicombe and Tony Benn to come along and talk about their lives in politics.

CHAPTER 26
OH YES IT IS

"Lionel Blair always says that he is 60 plus VAT. But he has the energy of men half his age. He is a tremendous raconteur, with a wealth of stories to tell, and is one of life's entertainers."

I adore pantomime. Absolutely adore it. As I said previously, my first one was with Lionel Blair and Rod Hull in Reading. Rod was one of the most naturally funny men I ever met – he was hysterical. I was so sorry when his life fell apart, losing almost all of his money on a property deal that went belly up. I wrote to him at the time to sympathise with his plight and was staggered when he came back to me and told me that I was the only person who had written to him. I suppose it is at times like that when you find out who your friends are.

Lionel was, and is, a larger than life character who lives for show business. With Lionel, age is just a number – he always says that he is 60 plus VAT. But he has the energy of men half his age. He is a tremendous raconteur, with a wealth of stories to tell, and is one of life's entertainers. He and his sisters used to sing to people in the bomb shelters during the Second World War – as if it weren't bad enough that you might lose your house to a German bomb, you then had to listen to Lionel and Joyce singing and dancing!

Lionel taught me well and gave me a piece of advice that I have carried with me ever since. He said: "If you are in panto and you are playing the part of an immortal you have to remain in character throughout the show because the children believe in you totally. When you are playing the part of the Fairy Godmother, for instance, you have to be her absolutely."

He also pointed out that panto was usually the first experience people have of coming to the theatre, and he was absolutely right. "So it is vital that you make it as marvellous as you can, and then it will stick with them and they will want to come back again and again." And he was absolutely right.

On my first night I was waiting to go on and I was incredibly nervous, just as I always am. Standing beside me was a young girl who was playing the part of one of the Babes in the Wood, and she turned to me and asked: "Is this your first panto?"

"Yes," I replied.

"Mmm, it shows."

And with that, off she went on to the stage, leaving me to think: "Bloody hell, that was a five year old!"

I was hooked right from the start, and I admit that part of the attraction is that it pays extremely well, which is the reason that so many top stars do it. And it is fun.

In saying that, panto is also extremely hard work. We do two shows a day and it is always very hot and sweaty – a great way of keeping fit actually. But it gives me the opportunity to dance and sing, which are two things I love to do.

You look out into the auditorium and I defy anybody not to be moved by the look of wonder on the faces of the children who come along with their parents. They are absolutely entranced by it, and get swept along with the whole thing. When you get an audience full of five year olds you find yourself wondering how it is possible that they can make as much noise as they do. They scream for almost the entire show, but they sit there believing everything that is happening on stage. It is glorious.

Adelaide, my grand-daughter, had been along to see me in panto in Norwich and afterwards she said: "Can you do magic Granny?"

"No darling, I can only do it while I am on stage."

"But why can't you do it here?"

"Because I don't have any powers here. I only have powers when I am wearing the costume and I am on the stage."

Many theatres rely on panto to make them enough money to carry on for the rest of the year. And the same thing applies to a lot of actors – appearing in panto is what keeps them going for another year. Just think about how many actors and actresses there are scrambling around looking for parts, and you will quickly realise what a difficult profession it is. So much of it is about being in the right place at the right time, being seen by the right person, whether that be a director or an agent.

Perhaps the best thing of all about panto is that you get the opportunity to fly. By that, I mean that you are suspended on a wire, high above the stage, looking down on everybody else.

My first experience of it was in *The Wizard of Oz* at Cambridge Corn Exchange. The director originally told me the show would not involve any flying, but then, a few days later, he had changed his mind and told me: "Liza you probably will be flying, but don't worry about it. It is a piece of cake."

So they set up the wires and pulleys and flew me from the back of the Corn Exchange on to the stage, 150 feet away. So I had my harness on and I was about 40 feet up in the air and because I had never done it before, I was spinning round and round in circles, screaming: "No way. I can't do this. I can't do this. You will have to phone my agent."

I seemed to spend quite a lot of time screaming. But then I realised that the key was to 'swim' in the air, using your core muscles to control what is happening. You have to be pretty fit.

The harness was extremely uncomfortable. Remember that I was already wearing a huge costume, and then I had to cope with the harness as well. I discovered that padded cycling shorts were the answer, and now I swear by them. They cut out all the chaffing that used to go on. In those days, there were straps everywhere, and it was extremely uncomfortable, like a form of torture. Now, the harness simply goes around your waist. And when I first started flying, there was only one wire, but now there are two, and it makes everything much easier.

I know that people probably think of me as somebody who usually plays goody two shoes-type parts, but my role in The Wizard of Oz was as the Wicked Witch of the West and it was great fun to play. I had a big pointed hat, a broomstick and I spent half the show cackling away. At one point I had to come in from the back of the theatre and the only way to do it was to go outside and walk along the street before coming back in through the main entrance – so there I was, in full costume, and nobody ever took any notice of me. It was as if it was perfectly normal to see a woman dressed as a witch going for a walk.

It was great to play a baddie and to make everybody hiss and boo. It is what pantomime is all about. And the better you are in the part, the louder the hissing and booing.

CHAPTER 27
THE ONE AND ONLY, PART ONE

"Rather sweetly, all the parts he does for me are described as 45-year-old women. I am flattered that he thinks I can still get away with it."

I have been incredibly fortunate to have worked with Alan Ayckbourn on a number of occasions. For me, he is Britain's greatest living playwright, and he may well be the best we have ever had.

I first met him in about 1974 through some friends, and my first experience of his work came through *The Norman Conquests* at Greenwich when they did all three plays that make up the trilogy in one day. It was one of the most extraordinary days of my life. I spent it with his first wife, Christine, and their two young sons. I remember that it was a scorching hot summer's day and we had a picnic on the grass.

The Norman Conquests were incredibly funny and featured an amazing cast that included Michael Gambon, Penelope Keith, Penelope Wilton and Tom Courtenay, none of whom were famous at the time – but they soon were after appearing at Greenwich.

I saw him off and on as a friend for many years, and would also travel to Scarborough to watch his plays. People seem to find it surprising that actors go the theatre, but why wouldn't we? We enjoy being entertained just as much as the man in the street does.

It was many years before I worked for him for the first time, and what an eye-opener that was. I admit that I was terrified at the prospect, mainly because I didn't want to disappoint him.

He would tell me what my character was thinking, so it was never just a case of learning the part – you had to try to get under the skin of who you were meant to be. You have to become the character.

He has now written a mind-boggling 75 plays, and each and every one of them is a gem, all written in 3D, all exploring every possible aspect of each and every character.

One of the reasons I enjoy doing his plays is that he writes great parts for women, and there are not many men who are capable of doing that. A lot of male writers will sit down and decide they are going to create a part for a woman and then simply put their point of view into the mouth of a female character – more often than not, you can tell just from reading the words that they have been written by a man.

And one of the reasons why there are so few great parts for women is that the industry is dominated by men – script-writers, authors, playwrights, directors, producers, the vast majority of them are male. It stands to reason, therefore, that two things will happen – most of the central characters they create will be men, and the women who appear in those productions tend to be walking cliches, stereotypes. As an actress, let me tell you that it can be extremely frustrating.

What is worse is that it is a modern phenomenon. If you look back at the old plays, the likes of Oscar Wilde and George Bernard Shaw did write cracking parts for women. Now, the female has become almost like a support act, put there to be decorative, but not to say very much of any great importance, and never to be more intelligent than the male. But real life just isn't like that. The days when a woman's place was tradition-ally seen as keeping the house for her husband have, thankfully, long since gone. There are very few jobs done by men that women cannot do equally as well.

And if you look around the world, some of the most powerful political positions are held down by women, who presumably have their husbands back home keeping the house for them! I wonder if Bill Clinton potters around the house with a pinafore and a feather duster while Hillary is jetting off to all parts of the world to help solve this crisis or end that conflict. It is an image that perhaps ought not to be dwelt upon for too long.

Ayckbourn's genius is in his ability to absolutely get into the mind of a woman. The fact that he started off as an actor may also have helped. I have never had to act out one of his scripts and think: "This just doesn't feel right. A woman wouldn't say that." On the contrary, he gets it exactly right. Every single time.

Oscar Wilde was also able to achieve this, but he was gay. In my view, Alan is that only straight playwright who possesses this gift – and it is a gift. If a character is to be believable, he or she must say things with which an audience can relate. Theatregoers are not stupid people – they know when something works, and when it doesn't.

He understands precisely how women think, so that when you are playing the role you know that it feels and sounds right. His characters also always have depth, an inner life if you like. In real life you can say one thing and be thinking another, and that is the feeling you get with his characters.

You never tire of exploring his characters because there is simply so much going on with them; they have tremendous depth. Remember that when somebody comes to the theatre, they need to believe in the people they are watching perform for them.

There may be a few people who come to see a play because Liza Goddard is among the cast, but I don't want them to see me on stage, I want them to see the person I have become. If they don't believe in the character, it doesn't matter who is on the stage because the whole thing would be a complete waste of time.

The Ayckbourn play *Communicating Doors* is about how people change you, and affect the direction your life takes. And in real life that happens too. There are certain people who take you down a path you would not otherwise have followed. Everybody can pinpoint a person who has changed their lives, whether it be a teacher, a work colleague or a partner. He describes *Communicating Doors* as an oil painting. It is very much in your face, a proper thriller that contains many farcical elements and then, at the end, it is very sad and leaves the audience with lumps in their throats. People come out of the theatre having had an amazing experience – they have laughed, they have screamed and, in all probability, they have cried. If not, I can guarantee that they have fought back the tears.

If *Communicating Doors* is an oil painting, *Life of Riley* is a water colour because it is far more gentle. It is about a group of people whose best friend has been given six months to live. The group start to wonder what might have happened had they taken a certain direction, even though it is too late to do so now. They each look back at the relationships they have had with him and examine how it has impacted upon their lives. It is sad, it is moving and it is very, very funny, all at the same time. And one of the quirks is that although the cast constantly refer to the central character, he never appears in the play.

One of the things that audiences love is to come to the theatre one night and see us perform *Communicating Doors* and then return the next night and see exactly the same cast in *Life of Riley*. It works so well because it is highly unusual for an audience to see actors play two entirely different roles on successive nights. I love it but it can be quite tiring.

When you are learning your lines, it is as if you are reading a real-life story because Alan will have characters saying something, and then going off on a tangent and talking about something, just the way we all do. You know what it's like – you will be having a conversation with somebody and something is said that reminds you of something else, and off you go down that road. How many times have we all stopped and said: "Now, where was I? What were we talking about?"

The audiences become totally rapt in it all because they can relate what they are seeing and hearing to their own lives. You can hear a pin drop in the theatre – right up until the second when a killer funny line is delivered.

All of Ayckbourn's plays have tremendous depth, and they are all hilariously funny as well. It is a strange thing though – there are many times when I have rehearsed an Ayckbourn play and believed that I have totally got what it is all about, and then you perform it in front of a live audience for the first time, you say a line, everybody in the audience laughs and you find yourself thinking: "What on earth are they laughing at?" And again, that is another mark of the man's genius. He knows when something is funny, and he knows precisely when the laughs will come.

Snake in the Grass, in which I appeared in Scarborough in 2008, is an Ayckbourn play about abuse – it is a dark subject matter, and there are

215

not many people who could tackle such a subject and do it justice anyway; there are even fewer who could tackle it and get away with a script that has countless hilarious lines. It is perhaps that humour that stays with people afterwards and gets them thinking in depth about the play and the subject matter it has tackled.

In Snake in the Grass he also introduces terror – he actually makes people jump out of their seats and scream. It is a rare gift.

Alan was effectively brought up by his mother after his Dad left home at an early age, and that may have something to do with his ability to empathise with women, both as performers and as an audience. He spent his formative years surrounded by aunts, and was a great listener and observer even back then.

He understands women completely, which is a rare trait in a heterosexual man. The result is that he has the women doing things in his plays that other writers would have the men doing. As a result, it is all the more believable. In *Communicating Doors*, for instance, the female characters have to drag off a dead body and fly off a balcony. In *Snake in the Grass*, one of the women is thrown down a well.

Don't run away with the idea that he only writes for women because that is not the case at all – he writes great parts for men as well. He is also pretty unusual in as much as there is never what you would term a 'star' part in any of his plays. It is all about developing a group of characters rather than allowing one person to play centre-stage. Everybody is as important as everybody else. The play is the most important thing and if the audience know that it has been written by Alan then they will also know that they are coming to watch a cracking show.

His name brings people through the door, especially if they know he has directed it as well, as happens in Scarborough. I have seen many of his plays directed by people who don't get what he is all about, and they have been terrible. If you are a director and you regard it as 'just a light comedy', it will be a disaster.

An Alan Ayckbourn play will only work when the cast and the director play it for real. If they play it for the jokes, it will never work. The Irish comedian Frank Carson says: "It's the way I tell them", and that is absolutely true and accurate of most things in life, but especially so of drama, whether it be a comedy or a tragedy, whether it be an Ayckbourn or a Shakespeare.

When he had his stroke in 2006 he thought that he would never be able to work again. Strangely enough, he told us that the thing he would have missed most was not the writing, but coming in for rehearsals. He has always loved mixing with actors. There are some directors who make you feel as if you are getting in the way and spoiling their set just by being there. Alan is not like that – he gets tremendous enjoyment from seeing us bring his characters to life. He adores the entire rehearsal process.

As he was recovering, he asked me to come to Scarborough and offered me a particularly challenging role in a play called *If I Were You* about a couple in a terrible relationship who spend the first half constantly arguing and bickering with one another. And then they wake up one morning and have swapped places, so in the second half I had to become a man. I started off as a downtrodden Scarborough housewife and then became a testosterone-empowered man, unable to work the Hoover and such things. Nobody else but Alan would have considered asking me to do such a part – and he has done that many times.

I have spent much of my career playing parts that haven't really stretched me – I suppose much of it had to do with the way I looked, as well as the fact that I became known as a comedy actress. And I also gained a reputation as somebody who didn't turn down work, mainly because I couldn't afford to.

If I Were You was outside my comfort zone and I found it terribly difficult, but that is beside the point. When we started rehearsals, Alan was quite frail but as each day went by he become more and more energised by the process, and I am convinced that it played a huge part in his recovery. Best of all, it proved that he still had what it took.

All his plays tackle serious subjects but always contain belting laughs. He says that he has spoken to people after they have watched one of his plays his who have said: "If I knew what I was laughing at, I wouldn't have laughed." As if they could control it.

He is also a great one for using throwaway lines in his work to pay homage to classic films, especially Hitchcock movies, and the audience always pick up on it.

Private Fears and Public Places is a bitter-sweet play about people trying to cope with city life. Alan lives in Scarborough – how does he know about city life? Trust me when I tell you that he does. One of his greatest gifts is probably an ability to observe people and places, to sit and watch life going by, and then to put it down on paper.

I often find myself wondering: "How does he know how these people who live alone in London feel? How does he do it?" I have learnt that it is best just to accept that he does know, and that is part of what makes him the man he is.

You will not be surprised to learn that he is also incredibly driven and focused. He tells a story of being disturbed by somebody as he was starting to write a play and when he finally sat down again in front of typewriter to begin tapping away he realised that the idea had gone from his head. As hard as he tried, he could not get it back, so he made up his mind right there and then that he would lock himself away and allow no outside distractions. When he got the idea for his 75th play, that is exactly what he did. He basically locked himself away in a room in his house and worked and worked until he had written it. Nobody is allowed to disturb him until he has finished writing. When he is in that mode, he adopts a lifestyle where food and sleep become necessary evils to fuel the brain and the body. I am certain that if he could do without both then he would until he emerged, triumphant, completed script in hand. He is helped throughout in this process by being looked after by Heather, his extraordinary wife.

As I understand it, most playwrights will go back through their work and change things over and over again. Not Alan. He is so particular about finding the right words in the first place that it would probably be impossible to improve on the finished product. Essentially, he makes his changes and does his rewrites as he goes along, and I sure he is unique in that. He knows precisely where every comma, full stop and semi-colon should go, and he drums the importance of that punctuation into our minds. There is a reason for it all.

He is also a technological wizard and when he wrote *Life of Riley*, he did all the sound effects and music on his computer. As if sitting down and writing a great play was not enough of a challenge. Before we opened the play he got very excited and told us all to come and listen to what he had done. It was fantastic.

I consider myself fortunate to regard him as a friend – he is quite the most wonderful raconteur I have ever met, with a wealth of anecdotes and funny stories to tell. When you are rehearsing for him he always makes a point of sharing some of these stories with us.

219

He tells one about Hermione Gingold, the sharp-tongued English actress who lived to be 90 and also happened to be the mother of Stephen Joseph, after whom the theatre in Scarborough is named. One night Alan and Stephen went back to Stephen's house and the housekeeper served them all some soup.

"Did you get this soup out of a can?" Hermione asked.

"No ma'am, I made it myself."

"Excellent. It's almost as good you know."

I have spent a good deal of time working at the Stephen Joseph theatre in Scarborough, and I just love it to bits. It is true theatre-in-the-round, where the stage is a circle, surrounded by the audience. There is seating for more than 400 people. The theatregoers feel that they are part of each performance, especially the ones who get to sit in the front row – they could reach out and touch the actors if they were so minded. A lot of actors don't like the round because they can't play practical jokes on their fellow performers.

Most of us cannot understand why there is not a theatre-in-the-round at the National Theatre in London because it is the purest way that we can possibly deliver our art. It goes back to the days when we all used to sit around the fire telling stories, and it is incredibly inclusive. It is frightening for actors, especially youngsters who have never experienced it before, because we are utterly exposed. There is no hiding place, which is why it is so important to become the character that the author has written for you – you cannot let your guard down for a second.

With a traditional stage, there is always the backdrop to give you some protection – nobody can see you from the back, or from the sides.

From an actor's point of view, it is about as good as it gets because you get instant feedback. In saying that, a lot of actors enjoy playing practical jokes on their fellow performers and they don't like the round because it is impossible to do that.

You just know when they are enjoying themselves. The only downside comes when somebody in the audience decides that they want to unwrap a sweet – people always think that it is best to do this slowly, but that is actually the worst thing they could do because it seems to go on forever, and because we as performers are so close, we are often tempted to say: "Excuse me, but will you either just unwrap that sweet and put it in your mouth, or will you put it away?"

It is like when you come home late at night and try to creep around the house so as not to wake anybody up, but all that you succeed in doing is creating lots more noise because the floorboards seem to creek more loudly than normal and every sound seems to be exaggerated.

It was the first theatre-in-the-round in Britain, and was established by Stephen Joseph in 1955 on the first floor of Scarborough's public library. The theatre flourished and in 1976 moved to a temporary home on the ground floor of the former Scarborough Boys' High School, where it remained until 1988, when the Odeon cinema closed and Ayckbourn, then the theatre's long-standing artistic director, identified it as the perfect venue.

Apart from the theatre-in-the-round, it has The McCarthy, a 165-seat end stage/cinema. The building also contains a restaurant, shop, and full front-of-house and backstage facilities.

The round boasts two important technical innovations: the stage lift, facilitating speedy set changes, and the trampoline, a Canadian invention which allows technicians easy access to the lighting grid.

When Joseph died, he left his home to the housekeeper who had looked after him, and Alan and Heather bought it from her. They lived in a flat and the housekeeper kept the rest, where she remained until she died. By that time, Alan was enjoying tremendous success and every time he came into serious money he would buy the house next door, until he ended up with four adjoining properties in the heart of Scarborough.

He then bought what used to be a Victorian school, so ended up owning just about half the street, and he turned the school into a rehearsal room, and I am here to tell you that it boasts the best views of any rehearsal room anywhere in the world – it looks out onto Scarborough bay, and the sight that greets you the first time you see it is quite breathtaking. I never tire of it. The wonder is that any work ever gets done because the distraction is there all the time.

The views from his house are exactly the same, and they change as the day passes. When darkness falls, you look out and see thousands upon thousands of twinkling lights. It is magical, and it makes you realise why he would never want to leave Scarborough. Alan has also had a small cinema built in the basement of the building, and he regularly shows films for the cast of his plays. It is a perfect way to while away a couple of hours. And he owns some classic black and white movies, including Laurel and Hardy's classic attempt at moving a piano up a flight of stairs. Until I watched it at Alan's, I had forgotten just how many gags, both visual and verbal, that film contained. When the films are finished, we have tea. What a wonderful life!

The likes of Laurel and Hardy, Buster Keaton and Harold Lloyd are Alan's heroes. He is potty about them.

Alan's wife Heather is an amazing woman, so much so that I, a friend, want to clone her and rent out the clones. She is his rock, and is completely devoted to him and to the theatre. Heather arranges his life in the most perfect way. The house is always perfect, the food is always the best, she is a wonderful hostess and she cares about everybody, and I do mean everybody. She is also a highly intelligent woman who knows all his plays backwards – she actually started out as an actress, and a very fine one too.

Now, hopefully, you will have some understanding of why I think so highly of Alan – if you have never been to see one of his plays I would urge you to put it on your 'to do' list as soon as possible. I promise that you will not regret it.

CHAPTER 28
THE ONE AND ONLY, PART TWO

"Phil had a truly wonderful way with horses, quite unlike anything I have ever seen before from any other human being. He was actually a horse whisperer before there was such a thing."

If Alan Ayckbourn has been the biggest influence on my professional life, there was another man who had a huge impact on my personal life.

When I was the 'victim' on *This is Your Life*, I mentioned that, at the end of the show, Sophie was led out on her horse by Phil Gardner. He was a constant in my life for a very long time, and I struggled to work out the best way of doing him justice here. In the end, I came to the conclusion that it was best to devote a chapter to a very, very special man.

Phil became a friend of my parents when I was just six months old and we lived in Farnham. Phil had his own riding school and was a champion showjumper from the age of nine, so it was natural that they would become friends. He also owned some racehorses and he would train them by putting complete beginners on their backs and riding round the lanes, for mile after mile. He had the fittest racehorses you have ever seen.

Phil had a truly wonderful way with horses, quite unlike anything I have ever seen before from any other human being. If you ever saw that wonderful film *The Horse Whisperer*, starring Robert Redford, you will get an idea of the sort of empathy he had for these magnificent creatures. He was actually a horse whisperer before there was such a thing.

One day, Dad went for a ride at Phil's riding school and was given a grey mare to take out.

Phil looked at Dad and thought: "Yes, this man can ride. He knows what he is doing on a horse." When my father returned the horse, Phil put it in a field and another horse wandered over to it, kicked it and broke its leg. Phil had to go into the house, return with a handgun and shoot the poor horse, and he was devastated. He never forgot my father – an hour's ride had cost him one of his favourite animals.

Despite that, Phil and Dad had an instant connection and became firm friends. Yes, the mutual interest was horses and riding, but they also shared much more in common.

There was nothing Phil did not know about horses, although even he would admit that he was not very good with people. But you always knew where you stood with him because he was very down to earth and called a spade a spade.

He taught my sister and I to ride when we were very young. I remember spending hours trotting round his field on horseback, crying my eyes out, and he would say: "For God's sake Liza, just shut up and keep trotting. What's the matter with you girl?" I should say that I had no stirrups, which was agonisingly painful. I didn't realise it at the time, but what he was doing was teaching me to ride properly, to get a feel for the horse and to learn all about balance. If let your concentration slip for even a split second while riding without stirrups, you will very quickly find yourself on the ground wondering what on earth has just happened.

We seemed to spend a lot of our childhood being shouted at by Phil and I suppose that, by rights, I should have hated him, but the reverse was true. I adored the man and looked up to him. I went for lessons every week and gradually became more proficient and as I became more proficient, so I began to really enjoy it and look forward to it.

He never married, and back then still lived with his mother. He had lots of girlfriends, but his horses always came first, and the women in his life could not cope with being second best.

He always had what he called a 'house cow', which had been bought purely and simply for its milk. I tasted fresh milk for the first time in my life at Phil's and thought: "This is amazing." It tasted completely different to the stuff we used to get from a bottle.

Phil and my parents used to go to hunt balls and suchlike together, but he would often leave the ball because he said that he had to go back and look after his horses – if he had a girlfriend with him, and he usually did, you can imagine how she would feel.

He was an extraordinary man and an extraordinary human being, the sort of friend who would do anything for you, who would give you his last penny if he thought it would help you.

Years later, when my parents returned from Australia, he sold them his old family home in Wrecclesham, and so the friendship was rekindled. When I moved back in with my parents from London, it was this house where I lived. Phil's Aunt Joan was a close friend of Julie Andrews' family. Her parents were performers and when they were on the road, Aunt Joan used to look after Julie and actually taught her to dance.

Phil used to provide the horses for lots of films and television programmes and they were always incredibly well trained animals. Some trainers used cruel methods to train their horses, but not Phil, although he did used to shout at them sometimes, and they would always respond to his voice. He used to say: "If you know exactly what you want you can transmit it to them. And you have to give them a routine, so they always have get their meals at the same time every day. If you look after a horse, it will look after you in return."

He used to take them to London, into television studios to appear on live shows – don't forget that this would have involved bright lights, extreme heat and loud audiences, but they were never spooked by any of it and took it all in their stride.

There was a live production of *Tale of Two Cities* which involved a major battle scene – if anything was going to faze the horses, it would have been that, but it never did. There were extras everywhere, scenes of pitched battles being filmed and guns and cannons going off, and through it all were Phil's magnificent horses. Of course, health and safety simply wouldn't allow it today, and they would probably be right – scenes like that should not have been filmed inside a studio.

They even filmed opera live back then, including *The Girl Of The Golden West* which featured an opera singer who had never been on a horse in his life and wasn't especially keen to do it, but he was required to do a scene that involved galloping at full pelt on horseback at Frensham Pond.

"Don't worry, you'll be fine. I've got an idea," said Phil. Without a word of a lie, he tied the singer on to the horse. Basically, he took a piece of rope, attached it to the singer's legs and fed it underneath the horse; Phil was riding another horse beside the singer and he had an assistant riding a horse on the other side, and all three galloped on as fast as they could, with Phil holding the rope on one side, his assistant holding it on the other, the singer performing an aria and everybody else with their hearts in their mouths, praying that Phil had tied the rope tight enough so that the singer wouldn't fall off.

Because I trusted his judgment totally, I asked him to help me each time I wanted to buy a horse, and he always produced the animal that was perfect for me. When I lived in Surrey I had a big Hanoverian horse that I had to re-home when Alvin and I split up because I'd had to move into a smaller house in Farnham and vowed that I would never have another horse. Phil found a home for her, and then he announced that he had found me another horse, whose name was Minnie.

"But Phil I don't want another horse just now."

"Yes you do Liza. Of course you do."

Unsurprisingly, he persuaded me to go and have a look at her with him and she was completely mad. Her owners couldn't catch her, even in the stable, and it was blindingly obvious that she was terrified. Eventually they caught her and the man climbed up on her back and she immediately bolted.

"Oh, she's perfect for you Liza. Perfect."

"What? They couldn't catch her, and she ran off the moment he got on."

"That's because he can't ride, and she knows he can't ride so she doesn't want him on her back. It will be different with you – you just see if I am not right."

He was right, so much so that she turned out to be the best horse I ever owned. He looked after her for me and I ended up buying a house nearby so I could literally walk up the lane, saddle up and go for a ride. He saw something in that horse that nobody else could see – the previous owners couldn't give her away. In the end, I could trust her with my life.

We used to go out for miles together, and quickly established a bond. We even managed to teach her to walk into my horse trailer – eventually. It took months because she was so frightened but eventually she trusted me sufficiently to realise that nothing bad would befall her if she walked in.

After that happened, I could load up horse and trailer, put all the dogs in the car and we would all head off and then go riding for three or four hours and forget about all the stresses and strains of everyday life. On horseback, I am able to empty my head of all thoughts and simply take in the scenery and breathe in all that glorious country air. It is so invigorating, and remains one of the reasons why horses have played such an important part in my life, and will always continue to do so.

Once we had finished our ride, I would put her back in the horse trailer, head back to Phil's, have a cup of coffee, tell him where I had been and then head home feeling as high as a kite. How I wish I had written down some of the words of wisdom that he used to impart. He was a great philosopher, but all his stories related to horses. That may sound a bit flaky, but it all made perfect sense. Phil Gardner was one of the wisest people I have ever met.

I was fairly low when I first moved back to Farnham after my split with Alvin, and Phil was a great help to me. Not only was he good with horses, but he was also good with children and teenagers. Sophie was eight at the time and Thom was 14, which was a tricky age to be going through all this upheaval. Fortunately, we also lived quite close to my mother, so if Thom and I fell out, as we did quite often, he would simply jump on his bike and ride off to see her. Just as he would storm off, I would pick up the phone, call Mum and say: "I think Thom's on his way. We've had a row."

The house I bought in Farnham was a small one because, once again,

I was worried about whether I would be offered any work, and I also had this theory that if I lived in a small house then I wouldn't need to work so hard because I didn't have such a large mortgage to pay. But, as has happened so often in my career, we had no sooner moved than the offers of work started to pour in once more, starting with *Give us a Clue*, followed by *Woof!*

When David and I first moved to Norfolk, Phil came to visit us to check out the area – not for our benefit, but for Minnie's. "Oh yes Liza, this will do nicely for her." Inevitably, the time came where the poor old girl had to be put down and so did Willow, who was Sophie's horse. It was a heartbreaking time for me and I made up my mind that I couldn't go through it again. If you are an animal person, whether it be a cat, a dog, a horse or whatever, when they die it can be like losing a member of the family – especially with a dog, you walk into a room expecting him or her to be following you, or you come home and expect them to bound to the front door to greet you, and every time that doesn't happen, it reminds you of what has happened, and it hurts.

I told Phil that I had reached the end of the road as far as owning another horse was concerned but then Sophie got another one, and when David and I moved to the cottage we live in now, I discovered that the people who had lived in it before us had also had a horse, but I was convinced that our garden wasn't big enough.

Then we went on holiday to Connamarra in Ireland on holiday. Through a friend of mine I had read a book called Errislannan by an artist whose name was Alannah Heather – it purported to tell the story of her upbringing but was in fact the story of Ireland really. Her family had lived in Errislannan for hundreds of years, so she had the full story of the famine, as experienced by the people who starved when the potato harvest failed. People would climb into coracles and row over to Clifton to sell whatever they could and if the weather was too bad for them to set out they would simply turn their coracles around and sleep beneath them.

She also knew all about The Troubles through the eyes of people who had lived in this little village on the west coast of Ireland and had been through it all, who had family or friends who had been killed.

We visited Errislannan while we are holiday – pioneering aviators Allcock and Brown made their historic landing in a field there. We met a lady called Mrs Brooks, who bred Connamarra ponies, so I thought that it would be rude not to have a ride on one of them. It was a beautiful pony and it was a glorious day, and when I dismounted I was told: "He's for sale, if you are interested."

"Please don't tell me that. I am not interested at all."

"Well if you don't want him, he will only end up going to the meat (slaughterhouse)."

"Please don't. We have just moved and I don't need a horse or want a horse. It's the last thing I want. Anyway, I've got nowhere to keep it."

Then Sophie informed me that there was a place not 20 minutes from where we lived that charged just £20 a week. "You have to get stuck in and do the work yourself – all you get is a field and room in a stable, so you would have to feed him and muck him out, but you are not going to be working as much, so you may as well take him."

I forgave Sophie her impudence at assuming that the work would dry up for me, and started to think seriously about it, but then it dawned on me that it would cost a fortune to bring him over to Norfolk – considerably more that he would cost to buy. So, reluctantly, I said no for what I thought was the final time, and removed all thoughts of this wonderful animal from my head.

The next thing was that the phone rang and a voice on the other end said: "Oh to be sure, it'll be no bother to be bringing yon horse to England. I've got a lorry."

And that was how I came to own another horse, called Tufty. When he came off the lorry, he had a luggage label tied into his mane. Typically Irish. I got him in 2007 and he is another terrific animal although I cannot ride him on his own; he needs to go out with somebody else.

One of the things I learnt from Phil was the importance of living for the moment, and not dwelling on past mistakes – you can't do anything about the past, but there are certain things you can do to control your destiny. When I ride my horse or, believe it or not, when I am mucking out, I live in the moment – mind you, when you are shovelling horse dung, you don't have much choice but to concentrate fully on the task in hand.

Whenever I wasn't working I would spend hours riding and then sitting in Phil's kitchen, chewing the fat, listening to his stories and his thoughts on life. He had retired when he was 55, selling the riding school land to Wimpey for something like £300,000, which was a fortune in those days.

After my father died following a heart attack in 1992, Phil assumed a whole new importance in my life. I suppose you could say that he became a substitute father to me. With people him you just assume that they are going to be around forever. He was a strong, healthy man, as fit as a flea and I was certain he would live to be 90 at least, but tragically, he was only 72 when he, too, passed away, claimed by prostate cancer. That was a great loss in my life. His death broke my heart.

He would also have been able to sort out Tufty's reluctance to go out on his own in a trice.

Because I ended up working so hard in 2009 and 2010, I have had to get somebody else to help me out with Tufty as I was away from home for so much of the time, so a girl called Alex looks after him for me. It meant that when I had a day off I didn't have to spend it all mucking out at the other stables. As an added bonus, when I want to ride Tufty, Alex comes with me.

I have also become something of a fair-weather horsewoman, and I just hate riding in the rain because all my gear gets wet and then everything has to be dried and oiled before you can use it again, so nowadays I tend to restrict my riding to the summer months.

Another long-term friend and mentor is Elizabeth Bell, an actress I first met in 1972, and who probably knows me better than anybody else.

She has been with me through all my highs and lows, personally and professionally, and is a great one for straight talking. If ever I go to see her and pour my heart out to her and she felt that I was being melodramatic, she would bring me crashing back to earth with: "Oh Liza, stop being such an arse." And so you know what? She was always right.

These are people you talk to when you are low, treat as a sounding board if you want a second opinion, somebody to stay with when you need a bit of company, somebody to celebrate with when something good happens, somebody who is truthful, who will tell you what is best for you, not what they think you might want to hear. These are people who you think will always be there, and you wonder how you could possibly live your life if they weren't around anymore. They know you so well that they will always tell you things as they really are.

Lizzie is as wise as Phil was in all those respects – a very, very important person in my life.

CHAPTER 29
AN ACTOR'S LIFE FOR ME

"A friend of mine was rehearsing a play and her director gave everybody crayons and had asked all the cast to draw pictures that represented the characters they were playing."

Some people think that being an actor is a glamorous existence. It isn't. There are hundreds, maybe even thousands, of us who spend our lives 'resting'. No matter how you choose to describe it or dress it up, if you are 'resting' then you are out of work.

Of course there are a chosen few who make vast sums of money from starring in popular TV series or, if they are incredibly lucky, from appearing in films. They are household names, and the sums they earn provide them with the luxury of being able to pick and choose the roles that they want to play. If a script comes along and they really don't fancy it, they will say no.

But most actors are not that lucky and have to take any and all work that comes along. And while they are waiting for that part to arrive, they have to take on a variety of jobs. Some work in shops, others work behind bars and others work as waiters and waitresses.

Please don't get the wrong idea. I am not complaining and, indeed, I have been extremely fortunate because I have always been able to find work. You never know when it is all going to dry up, when the casting directors and agents are going to stop calling, so I have always found it fairly difficult to turn work down.

Apart from anything else, I need to keep earning. I suppose that I could retire, but it would mean being more careful with money.

Actors enjoy a good laugh, often at the expense of their fellow professionals. The worst to work with are the ones who go out of their way to try and make you laugh while you are on stage. The chief culprit in my experience was Stephen Moore, who starred in *Rock Follies* and is one of our finest stage actors. He was a nightmare, an absolute nightmare.

The late Christopher Cazenove was another, but poor old Chris did it unintentionally. He had this habit of getting his words muddled up or he would come out with the wrong line or the wrong word, so instead of saying: "Would you like a slice of Dundee cake?" he would actually say something like: "Would you like a slice of Danish cake?" I know that it doesn't sound funny but when you are on stage and somebody says something that is so obviously incorrect, it can be very, very difficult to keep a straight face, especially when the other actor realises what he has just done and starts pulling funny faces at you. And, of course, there is nothing worse than an 'in' joke, something that the cast get but the audience does not.

On a traditional stage, you can briefly turn away from the audience so that they don't realise you are laughing – but you can't do that in the round because the audience sees everything.

As an actor, when you make a mistake you tend to beat yourself up over it, but there is really no need because as long as you have managed to keep going, the chances are that the audience will not have the first idea

235

that you have dropped a clanger. They haven't read the script, they haven't seen the play before and they will probably never see it again. Sometimes even your fellow performers don't know because they are so focused on their own lines.

Alan Ayckbourn always knows when you get a word wrong though – he is a perfectionist who prides himself in his use of words, and every one is chosen for a reason. If you make a mistake in front of him he winces, as if you have hit him. It is understandable because his plays are like his babies. He is also very particular about punctuation – and it is only right that he should be.

If he puts a comma in his script, it is a sign that you have to take a pause. It helps with the rhythm of the piece, and it also assists us as performers with our breathing because when you take a brief pause, that is the moment when you can also take a breath.

In saying that, he is incredibly patient with us all.

A friend of mine was rehearsing a play and his director gave everybody crayons and had asked all the cast to draw pictures that represented the characters they were playing. When I heard this story I thought: "Well I would rather be rehearsing." I told Alan the story and he thought it was terribly funny and a pretty strange thing to do.

He went away and decided to draw his own picture. In the top corner was a character who was the writer and in it he was tearing his hair out, throwing pens and things around and screaming: "Aaaaaarrrrgggghhhhh!"

There was another character at the bottom of the picture. It was the director, and he had this lovely beaming face, smiling happily. Alan loves directing and, despite everything, he loves actors. The people who work for him soon pick up on this, and that is why we would do absolutely anything for him. Without question.

When you know he is the theatre, that is the time when you tend to make mistakes because we all want it to be perfect for him and I suppose that we just end up trying too hard. All of us who come to Scarborough to appear at the Stephen Joseph theatre do so for Alan Ayckbourn. It is as simple as that. He used to run the theatre, directing and writing the plays that were performed on stage and even directing and writing the Christmas show.

To work with him is a unique experience, something that gets my juices flowing and reminds me why I do what I do.

As I have grown older, I have discovered that the roles available to me in TV have diminished. I console myself with the fact that there are still many classic roles that I could play. But as far as television is concerned, I might as well be dead and buried. For want of a better way of putting it, I believe it is a visual thing – if a director is looking for a central female character, it seems to me that looks are very important. In truth, that is nothing new – if you look back at all the classic Hollywood movies of the 1940s and '50s, the female leads were always stunningly beautiful women.

There were some notable exceptions. You would never describe somebody like Bette Davis as being beautiful in the classical sense, but what an amazing actress she was. She possessed a huge screen presence, and the atmosphere positively crackled when she appeared.

Today, there is an obsession surrounding television of trying to attract younger audiences, and casting directors have got it into their heads that if you want to pull in a younger audience, then you shouldn't give a part to anybody over the age of 40. It is, of course, totally unfair and thoroughly misguided. The older you get, the more life experience you pick up and the more you can bring to any part that you play. And as I have already said, I am convinced that they are whistling in the wind because the young people they are trying to target will not watch anyway.

I know how fortunate I have been. First of all there was *Skippy*, and then there were a host of series on British television. It all seemed so easy, and it never entered my head that it would come to an end. Please don't get the idea that I was blasé about it all or that I felt TV owed me some kind of a living, because nothing could be further from the truth. I was blessed.

But when I hit 50, the calls became fewer and further between, and the television parts started to dry up. I was still the same actress. In fact, I was older and more experienced, so I would argue that I was a better actress, but it seems that image is all. There was nothing I could do about turning 50. I thought I still looked pretty good for my age, and I would never resort to Botox or to having a facelift or anything like that.

Realising that I was 50 was a tough time for me, but perhaps that was as much because I was menopausal as it was because I realised that I'd reached a landmark birthday, a point from which the only way was down. At one stage I had a right good rage, where I asked: "Why can't I be in a television series now? Why can't I get something that gives me a nice fat pay cheque? I don't even need to be the star, just a regular part will do, something that pays sufficiently well to allow me to keep my house in Norfolk. Oh yes, and I don't want it to be too much hard work. It is not too much to ask is it?" Well apparently it was.

There weren't many parts for women of a certain age back then and because I didn't look like a 'mumsy Mum' nothing of that sort came my way – I didn't have grey hair and I wasn't plump. You get pigeon-holed, put in brackets, and it is tremendously unfair. I suppose that I was regarded as a ditzy blonde, but quite clearly, that is not a part you can play for ever.

There are exceptions to this rule, of course, and one of the most notable would be Joan Collins, who did some of her finest work after she turned 50. But she was an incredibly glamorous woman. Judi Dench, Helen Mirren and Dame Maggie Smith have also worked long past their 50th birthdays, but the point I am making is that these are notable exceptions.

There have been huge changes at the BBC. I remember when my father worked as a producer at the corporation, his office at the old television centre had linoleum on the floor, and everything seemed terribly basic and old-fashioned, even when it was new. Nowadays, at a time when they are meant to be cutting back, there are thick carpets on the floors and the furniture is all very modern and expensive. It does make you wonder: if they spend so much money on offices, does the output suffer as a result?

I know that most people look at the past through rose-tinted spectacles, but there is not the slightest doubt in my mind that while the BBC still produces lots of wonderful work, especially wildlife documentaries, its drama output has suffered horribly. And the same thing could be said of its comedy. The Beeb, remember, gave us *Only Fools and Horses*, *Open All Hours*, *Porridge*, *Citizen Smith*, *Butterflies*, *The Good Life*, *To the Manor Born* – the list is endless. In today's schedules, there is nothing to compare.

In my father's day, the BBC didn't pay anybody terribly well, and nobody complained because they regarded it is as an honour to work for or appear on the Beeb. And in those days, the money was spent on ensuring that the output was of the highest possible quality. I am not saying that they deliberately go out of their way to produce poor programmes today because that clearly isn't the case. But there are no longer what I would describe as flagship dramas, and that is a real shame.

I struggle to get my head round the fact that the so-called stars now get paid vast sums of money at a time when the quality of the programmes in which they appear has so clearly slipped. The money used to go into the programmes; now, it goes into the people. To me, that is the wrong way round.

I also wonder why the same faces appear in television drama. It seems they have identified a small pool of actors and have decided to give them all the plum roles. My own opinion is that viewers must surely get tired of seeing the same faces over and over again.

Apart from anything else, it sends out all the wrong signals. If you continue to draw from a small pool, you are effectively telling up and coming actors and actresses that they are wasting their time. It is sad but true that most young people go into the profession because they want to appear on television, but the opportunities are few and far between.

Audiences love to see fresh faces. We all like to be surprised.

There was a golden period during the 1970s and 1980s when we were producing classic TV situation comedies by the bucket load. The writing was fabulous and the actors who starred in the shows loved delivering the lines because they knew how funny they were. I was lucky enough to have appeared in a couple of those shows.

It is a very different story today, and I cannot understand why because the talent is still out there. I know lots of people who are still writing innovative, funny scripts – they send them off to the TV companies, and cannot even get arrested. I would love somebody to sit down and explain to me why that is.

Is it because the BBC and ITV don't want to pay big money to the stars? I doubt it. There was a time when the BBC would take a chance on a series; more often than not, those gambles paid off, so why on earth won't they do the same thing today? We have dozens of great comedy actors and actresses, so why not make the most of them?

The powers that be are taking bland, ordinary scripts and giving them to people they believe will make it funny – but they are not. For me and for any actor worth his or her salt, the script is the only thing. Do you believe that David Jason would have achieved the success he did had the scripts for *Only Fools and Horses* been poor? Of course he wouldn't.

John Sullivan produced some of the funniest scripts ever, but Jason definitely added the final magic ingredient with his portrayal of Del Boy, just as Nicholas Lyndhurst brought something special and unique to the part of Rodney. But without those incredible lines and visual gags, it wouldn't have lasted five minutes. And it has stood the test of time – if you sit down and watch an episode of *Only Fools and Horses*, you will find that it is just as funny today as it was when it was first broadcast.

Why do you think those old comedy series are still being shown? It's because they were funny. *Dad's Army* is another classic. When the platoon captured the German airman and he looks at Ian Lavender and demands to know his name and Captain Mainwaring intervenes with: "Don't tell him Pike," it is one of the greatest comedy moments.

My job as an actress is to take a script and turn the words into a believable person, somebody that the audience can relate to. Stand-up comedians are funny – well, most of them are. On the whole, actors are not funny. What we do is to take somebody else's wit and humour and bring it to life. If we do it properly, and if the words were funny in the first place, then the chances are pretty high that an audience will laugh. But that is my job; it is what I am paid to do, and if I don't have a script I may as well not bother.

Even the beloved Dame Judi Dench could not make a bad script good. Nobody could.

Television audiences are changing, and the programme-makers are doing little or nothing to take account of this or change it. Most viewers are middle-aged or elderly. The truth is that young people watch very little television, other than the likes of the *X Factor*.

Youngsters tend to download stuff onto their computers or watch programmes through things like iPlayer. They have becoming far more discerning than people of my generation ever were. If they are sitting in front of a TV, the chances are that they have a mobile phone stuck to their ear. I am not knocking it and I am not criticising them – it is just the way that things have moved on as a result of technology.

Why would they want to watch a brain-numbing programme when there is a personal best to be achieved on the latest computer game, or when there is a new CD by JLS to be listened to?

It is also a reality that there isn't enough quality drama around today. When I started working in British television you had the likes of *Play for Today*, some of which were and remain absolute classics, *Play of the Week*, *Play of the Month*, and *The Friday Play*. On top of that, you could regularly watch Shakespeare on television – not now though.

Working for the BBC in the late 1960s and into the 1970s was incredibly exciting because the corporation was a world leader and made some fabulous programmes.

One gets the impression now that the British television industry has almost become lazy. How many more reality TV shows can they make?

The thing is, of course, that reality television is cheap to make and it also tends to be fairly easy.

While the likes of the X Factor will always uncover some amazing talent, such as Leona Lewis and Alexandra Burke, the reason that it is so popular is because people want to watch those amazing auditions when individuals who cannot sing a single note in tune walk in and announce that they want to be the next Mariah Carey or Michael Buble and then proceed to screech and wail until that nice Simon Cowell puts them out of their misery.

Why don't the people who love these individuals stop them from making complete fools of themselves? Mind you, if they did then there would be no X Factor, would there? But viewers have always loved talent shows.

People also enjoy good stories – they love drama, and want to get involved with the characters, they want to find out what makes them tick and to work out which way a plot is going to go. If you put on a great drama, either a one-off or a series, viewers will flock to it and get hooked on it. If you are the BBC that can only be good news because it means you will probably be able to make money by selling it abroad, and if you are ITV it is good news because advertisers will be prepared to pay a premium for a slot during the commercial break if they know lots of people are tuned in.

Regional theatre is going through a great time at present. As I tour around the country I find myself playing to packed houses just about every single night because they know they are going to be entertained – they know they will have a good laugh or a cry, or that they will go home having been provided with food for thought.

When they switch on their TV and start flicking through hundreds channels they can only hope that they might stumble across something that they will be able to enjoy – and usually when they do, it will be something that was made 23, 30 or even 40 years ago.

It is not all bad. I love Strictly Come Dancing and would jump at it if I was ever invited to appear on the show. And Dancing on Ice is another show that I enjoy, although it seems altogether too dangerous to me.

I would never in a million years consider doing I'm A Celebrity Get Me Out Of Here because I couldn't bear the thought of eating those awful-looking bugs and grubs. Some of the bush tucker trials are simply beyond the pale. I am not too keen on the prospect of having hundreds of rats, spiders or snakes crawling all over my body either. I say I wouldn't consider it, but if they offered me, say, £60,000 then it might be very difficult to turn down. I look at some of the people who have appeared on the show and wonder what on earth has possessed them to agree to it.

I can understand that for some it might be a way to relaunch a career, to get themselves back in the public eye, but it is one heck of a gamble, and it could all backfire if the public decide that they don't actually like the real you.

When it was first screened it was good entertainment, but my view is that it has become increasingly cruel and horrible, although the 2010 series was better than it has been for years, chiefly because Shaun Ryder and Stacey Solomon were such wonderful characters. Stacey had to win, of course, because she is such a genuinely lovely girl. It is almost as if she has become a celebrity by accident.

I was never able to understand the attraction of Big Brother. Why would you want to tune in and watch people sleeping? And why is people arguing with one another considered to be entertainment? And it seems to go on for weeks and weeks.

I don't want to seem holier than thou because it is not as if I haven't done things throughout my career simply for the money. I wanted to be a classical actress and when I set off on that path it never crossed my mind that I would end up doing as many game shows as I did. I want to let you in on a little secret though – some people may look down their noses at celebrity game shows, but they are enormous fun to do, and I am proud of them.

CHAPTER 30
SOAP SUDS

"Why aren't you getting any telly? Well it might have something to do with the fact that you are never available because you are always working."

I remember asking my agent why I wasn't getting any television work. Back came the reply: "Why aren't you getting any telly? Well it might have something to do with the fact that you are never available because you are always working."

I couldn't argue with that, I suppose, but if the right parts had been coming along then I would have found the time, and the truth is that they were not.

I started in the theatre and I will continue there until nobody wants me anymore, and then I will ride off into the sunset on my horse. Every time I finish a run I think to myself: "Right that's it. I will never work again." But that hasn't been the case so far.

I am a big fan of *Coronation Street* which, for 50 years, has consistently delivered great storylines, laced with wonderful northern humour. It tackles all the big issues, but you always know that no matter how serious the subject matter, there will always be something to make you smile.

Taking *Coronation Street* as an example again, when a new family is introduced viewers will almost always take the view that the newcomers will not work. And yet, within a few episodes, it is like they have always been part of the fabric of the programme – it is part of the genius of the script-writers.

I have never been offered a part in a TV soap but I actually quite fancy it, even though many of my friends who appear in the soaps or have done in the past all say that it is incredibly hard work.

In *Coronation Street* they film around 15 scenes a day, every day, and I guess the most confusing thing for the cast must be the fact that these scenes can all be from different episodes so they have little or no sense of continuity. It is a very demanding schedule, especially when you consider that they now put out so many episodes a week, and still retain the quality for which it has always been so famous.

Many, many years ago I was working at the Granada studios, where *Coronation Street* is made. It was quite extraordinary – in one studio, Lord Olivier was filming *King Lear*, in another I was filming my programme, and in a third they were filming Corrie. And, of course, I got to hear all the stories. Back then, when it was just one episode a week, and they were famous for rehearsing things over and over until everybody felt they had got it right. The standards were incredibly high.

"You don't talk to the grand dames when you first come in to the show. You must wait for the likes of Pat Phoenix (Elsie Tanner) and Violet Carson (Ena Sharples) to talk to you. And woe betide anybody who sits in their seats," I was told. Pat was a prima donna, who used to flounce around in a fur coat. I don't think there are any prima donnas in the programme now, simply because they all understand that the Street is bigger than any of them.

Coronation Street produced a live episode to celebrate its 50th anniversary, and very good it was too, but the media made a huge fuss of the fact that it was being filmed live – back in the day, it was common for drama programmes to be filmed live, and nobody made a big deal of it because that was the norm. Don't think that I am yearning for a return to those days because although much of it was live, it was not all top quality.

Pat Phoenix came from rep – she knew what it was to perform in front of a live audience. And so did just about every other member of the original cast. And it shone through right from the start, which is just one of the reasons why it was so successful – that and brilliant scripts. It is a show with a fabulous reputation and everybody loves it and wants to appear in it. Just look at the people who have been guest stars – Sir Ian McKellern, Nigel Havers, Peter Kaye, even Status Quo and Prince Charles!

CHAPTER 31
WHATEVER GETS YOU
THROUGH THE DAY

"If you protect the tiny beetle it means you are protecting the next creature up the food chain, the one that eats the beetle to survive. And so it goes on."

When I spoke about Alvin, I made it clear that being a born-again Christian was not for me, but in 2007 I discovered shamanism, which has been a fantastic experience for me, and my plan is to become a shamanistic healer.

It is a belief that reveres everything and regards every living creature as being part of a whole entity. People, animals, trees, plant are all to be respected – I have found it easy to follow because, to me, it seems to go hand in hand with wildlife conservation, which is something in which I believe quite passionately. If you protect the tiny beetle it means you are protecting the next creature up the food chain, the one that eats the beetle to survive. And so it goes on.

It is an ancient way of life and beliefs, and I discovered it through reading Manda Scott's *Boudica* books, recommended to me by Sophie. We went along to one of her introductory courses – Sophie went first and came back raving about it, telling me that I had to go too. It is a marvellous way of looking at the world and of experiencing spiritual practice.

Like-minded people get together for weekends throughout the year, but it is not something that has taken over my life. We sit in a circle and talk and share experiences. What I get from it is a sense of spiritual fulfilment, and it suits me. It is a belief that was followed by the original tribes-people of America, and the Sami, who live in the Arctic Circle – in a nutshell, they believed that we are all connected to every other living thing in some way or another, something which was been borne out by quantum physics.

Manda is a remarkable woman. She is a vet, writer and climber, who was born and educated in Scotland. She trained at the Glasgow Vet School and now lives and works in Herefordshire, sharing her life with her partner, a spaniel and some chickens. She is known primarily as a crime writer. Her first novel, *Hen's Teeth*, described by Fay Weldon as 'a new voice for a new world', was shortlisted for the 1997 Orange Prize. Her subsequent novels, *Night Mares*, *Stronger than Death* and *No Good Deed*, for which she was hailed as 'one of Britain's most important crime writers' by *The Times*, are published by Headline.

The Boudica series were her first historical novels and she said that she was born to write them.

If you check out shamanism on the Internet, you will come across an explanation that goes something like this:

"Shamanism is a range of beliefs and practices regarding communication with the spiritual world, and a practitioner of shamanism is known as a shaman. Shamanism encompasses the belief that shamans are intermediaries or messengers between the human world and the spirit worlds. Shamans are said

to treat ailments/illness by mending the soul. Alleviating traumas affecting the soul/spirit restores the physical body of the individual to balance and wholeness. The shaman also enters supernatural realms or dimensions to obtain solutions to problems afflicting the community.

"Shamans may visit other worlds/dimensions to bring guidance to misguided souls and to ameliorate illnesses of the human soul caused by foreign elements. The shaman operates primarily within the spiritual world, which in turn affects the human world. The restoration of balance results in the elimination of the ailment.

"Shamanism is a 'calling'. Individuals who are 'called' typically experience an illness of some sort over a prolonged period of time. This illness will prompt the individual to seek out spiritual guidance and other shamanic healers. Such illnesses are usually not healed/curable by physicians and western medicine. The shaman heals through spiritual means that consequently affect the human world by bringing about restored health."

So there you have it. I would never get on my soapbox and tell you that shamanism is the answer to all our problems, although I am absolutely convinced that we all have a part to play in looking after our planet and the things that grow on it and the creatures that live on it. I appreciate and understand that different things work for different people.

I have spoken throughout this book about my passion for my work, but in recent years I have thought about cutting down my workload, and I have even considered retiring. If David and I cut right back then we could probably just about manage it. The thing is that acting, rehearsing, learning lines, it all keeps you young. I worked with Dora Bryan when she was well into her 70s, and she had the energy of a young girl and was still able to do the splits. It was amazing. June Whitfield is another.

When you hit your sixties, as I now have, you tend to reflect on what you have achieved, and I am fairly proud of my body of work. I regard by best television role as Philippa Vale in *Bergerac*, for all sorts of reasons – it was a character I was able to develop, viewers loved the uncertainty as to whether she and Bergerac would ever get together, and I loved working in Jersey with John Nettles. It was win-win all the way. How I wished that they had gone on to make a series built around Philippa – they tried to, but it never quite worked out.

As far as theatre is concerned, I regard my crowning glory as Alan Ayckbourn's *If I Were You*, the one in which I had to transform myself from a depressed, downtrodden northern housewife into her husband. Nobody else would ever have cast me in such a part, and it was a life-changing experience for me. The card I received from him in which he wrote 'I think you are a better actress than you believe that you are', gave me a lump in my throat when I read it and remains one of my most treasured possessions. For me, praise comes no higher.

CHAPTER 32
ANIMAL CRACKERS

"In the morning I would walk to the bus stop to go to school, and Sidney would come with me and make sure that I caught my bus safely. On his way back home he would call in and visit a couple of elderly ladies, whom he knew would give him a snack."

You will have realised by now that animals have played a major part in my life. I have owned a huge assortment of dogs, cats, geese, chickens, ponies and horses, and feel that they deserve a mention all to themselves, so here goes. I warn you now that it is a pretty formidable list, but they were all unique characters, all individuals, just as human beings are.

As a child growing up we had Bella the boxer and Cassie the pony, who was a lovely dun mare. You will remember that I told you we lived in a tiny shoebox of a house, but we had a field in the garden, which was where Cassie grazed.

Then we moved to Farnham, which was where I acquired Mousey, who was a Connemara pony – Phil Gardner found her for me, just as he found all the ponies in my life. At that time, my sister had a little Dartmoor pony. They were a great joy. We also had a black poodle called

Suzy; my parents had a friend who was a retired burglar – he married a very wealthy woman, so he didn't need to break into houses any more. But he said that poodles made the best guard dogs because they could not be bribed with food. If a stranger breaks into a house, a poodle will bark non-stop.

Oh yes, and then there was the goose. Sidney. He came to us as a gosling and from the very first day he would follow me wherever I went. In the morning I would walk to the bus stop to go to school, and Sidney would come with me and make sure that I caught my bus safely. On his way back home he would call in and visit a couple of elderly ladies, whom he knew would give him a snack.

Then he would go home until it was time to come and meet me off the bus. Now I know how crazy all of this must sound, but I swear that it is true. And woe betide me if the bus happened to be late for any reason – he would bite my legs all the way home to let me know he was upset with me.

When visitors approached the house, Sidney used to rush up to their cars and bite their tyres, forcing them to hoot their horns until one of us came outside to assure them that it was safe for them to get out. Once we were painting the house with pink paint, and Sidney discovered that he had a taste for it.

If ever we decided that we were going to have a picnic on the lawn, we would all creep outside, as quietly as possible and lay the cloth and all the food on the grass and then not talk to one another because as soon as he realised what we were doing he would rush up to us and start helping himself to the food, while dancing around flapping his giant wings in the air. He would drink tea and eat cake, just as if it were a perfectly normal thing for a goose to do.

Then my father had the brilliant idea to build a swimming pool in the back garden. Dad and a family friend dug a huge hole – to be fair, it really was very impressive. Rather than putting concrete down and laying tiles, Dad decided that plastic sheeting would be absolutely fine, so he duly lined it with plastic and then filled it up with the garden hose.

Sidney dived straight in and absolutely loved it – right up until the moment he nibbled a hole in the lining and all the water ran away, still with Sidney inside it. Of course he couldn't get out, so we had to get a ladder, drop it into what was left of Dad's swimming pool and rescue the goose. We were left with a huge gaping hole, and Dad never did do anything about it.

One of the worst things about moving to Australia was leaving all the animals behind, but we did find them all new homes. Mousey went to friends of my parents, and she lived to be 39, which is a ripe old age for a pony.

Almost as soon as we arrived in Sydney we started rescuing animals, starting with Poochie who was a cattle dog we found abandoned on the beach, and then there was Randy, who was half Labrador-half greyhound, and he was a nightmare. He attacked cars, he attacked people and he didn't even belong to us. We kept taking him back to his owner, who would swear at us and accuse us of stealing his dog.

"We are not stealing your dog. We are bringing him back to you. We don't even like your dog. He comes to our house, he fights with all the neighbours, chases all the cars, humps all the bitches in the neighbourhood and he steals food. We don't want him so will you please keep him in?"

But he kept coming back and, in the end, finished up living with us because it became the easiest option. I came home one day and discovered him lying at the side of the house in a terrible state – he had clearly been struck by a car and had then crawled into the garden. I had to carry him three miles to vet to have him stitched up. He ended up looking like Frankenstein's dog. But as soon as he had recovered, he was off chasing cars again.

I also had a horse called Boxer while we were in Australia. Incredibly, my sister even found a horse in the local shopping centre. I remember Mum being worried in case they still shot horse thieves in Australia!

Obviously, when I returned to England I didn't have any pets, for just about the first time in my life. But when my parents came home and moved back to Wrecclesham, we started getting more dogs.

There was Spot, a Jack Russell who was an amazing rat catcher. People would come and borrow her for a day or two and she would clear an entire barn of rats in no time at all and then she would come home and sleep for three days. I guess that chasing and killing rats was pretty exhausting work.

We also had an enormous Great Dane. There is actually no such thing as a small Great Dane. Most of these animals were given to us as rescue dogs, so they were extraordinarily badly behaved, especially when we first got them, but this one managed to eat the sofa. Mother came home from the shops, went into the lounge and initially thought it had been snowing indoors before she realised that what she was looking at was the stuffing from the sofa, scattered everywhere.

At that time we also kept lots of chickens, who would come charging into the house, and we had to throw them out the window to get them back outside. It must have looked like a scene from a cartoon.

When I moved to Muswell Hill I got Sadie, a whippet who had been rescued by a friend of mine. This poor little dog had been treated really badly by her previous owner. Then I married Colin and we had another whippet, called Monty. Next came the most beautiful red setter called Cleo. We went to a pub for lunch one day and it was a lovely day so we sat outside and I was admiring Cleo.

"What a lovely dog you have," I said.

"Well you can have it."

"Yes, yes. Very funny."

"No, no, you can have the dog."

And so it was that we went home with a red setter. When Colin and I split up, he kept Cleo because he adored her, and she lived to be a great old age.

I bought a horse called Olive, a Hanavarian, after riding her at a school and being told she was for sale. "No no, please don't tell me that. I really don't want to know about buying horses just now." But of course I did buy her, and ended up moving to Surrey.

She had to have a friend, so Phil found Domino. Horses and ponies cannot live on their own – they need to have company because they are social creatures who love to interact.

Next up were two Shetland ponies, which I picked up cheaply. They turned out to be pregnant so we ended up with four Shetland ponies, Rhylla, Georgy, Star and Tompet. Rhylla went to Sue Jameson's daughter and became a terrific competitor, ending up at the Horse of the Year Show competing in Shetland racing. Georgy went to a friend, and Star ended up in Cornwall with a friend of Phil Gardner who had a Shire horse farm, and Tompet went to a friend who moved to Devon.

It was while we were in Surrey that I got Gertrude, the retriever who starred with me in the West End. Gertrude had to have a friend (obviously) so we went to Battersea Dogs Home and came home with

Gracie, a little black dog who was an absolute delight. Thumbprint, who was a kitten from a friend's litter, arrived as Gracie was having a phantom pregnancy and had milk, so he suckled from her and for the rest of his long life he looked on her as his mother and he was her baby. Thumbprint was a fierce hunter who was always bringing in dead rabbits or rats.

We also had Frederique, a miniature daschund who ruled the roost, but she was another lovely little dog. At one time while I was living in Surrey I had nine dogs. It was all a bit silly.

I upped sticks again, and this time it was to The Bourne in Farnham. You will recall that Phil once more decided that I needed a horse, so I ended up with Minnie. And then all these dogs started appearing, starting off with a deer hound, called Annie who had been bred by a friend, and my sister had Flora, who was Annie's sister. Next up was Clark Kent, a lurcher. I was doing a charity ball for what is now called the Dogs Trust, but was the Canine Defence League back then and Jilly Cooper said: "Oh he's a lovely dog Liza. I'd take him if I could, but I can't." So I did instead.

There was also Rosie, the Jack Russell, who bit everybody, and then Phil gave me Ceaser, a kitten found under a stable. He was a ginger tom, and he was petrified when we first got him. He was also wild by instinct but Sophie tucked him under her arm and, aged just eight years old, she somehow managed to tame and train him. He became the biggest laziest cat in the world and ate everything that Thumbprint brought in.

When we first moved to Norfolk we rented a house from Dinsdale Landen, for ten weeks and Thumbprint loved it there. When we moved to Wicken Pond Farm, he went missing and after a week I assumed he'd been run over, but then we got a phone call from the farmer whose land was adjacent to Dinsdale's house and he said: "Have you left a cat here?" It was Thumbprint. He had travelled ten miles across unfamiliar country to get there. We went and got him and kept him in, but off he went off again and this time he had a fight with what must have been an enormous rat, and needed stitches and a drain in his head. We thought that would cure him of his wandering bug, but he soon vanished again, so I phoned the farmer and asked him to keep an eye out for Thumbprint. Sure enough, he turned up ten days later and this time I put him in kennels for two weeks and then shut him in at home for three weeks and that eventually did the trick.

When we were first looking round the house at Wicken Pond Farm there was a lovely golden retriever called Ben and Sophie and I were chatting to the woman who was selling it, while David was away talking to the man about tractors and things. Once again, I admired the dog and she told me: "We are going to have him put down because we can't have him where we are moving to."

I couldn't bear the thought of it, and told her I would take him, and didn't mention it to David. It ended up being one of those things that the longer you leave it unsaid, the more difficult it becomes to admit. We were having lunch with friends one day and one of them asked: "How many dogs have you got now?"

Sophie, who was with us, said: "Six."

"Six?" said David.

"Yes. There's Gertrude and Gracie, Annie and Clark Kent, Puppy Wuppy and Ben."

"Who's Ben?" asked David.

"Oh sorry darling, I forgot to tell you. Ben's the dog that comes with the house we are buying."

He was a great dog who had spent most of his time outdoors, and he loved being in the car. I had an old Daihatsu van that I used to take the animals to and from the beach and Ben used to sleep in it. People would arrive and he would bark, get out and have a sniff around and then clamber back into the van. When he had to be put down, we asked the vet to do it in the van.

Then there was Bebe, who belonged to an Animal Aunt called Anna, but she fell in love with Sophie so Anna ended up giving her to Sophie. We were going on holiday to Cyprus and when we came back Anna told us that Bebe jumped onto Sophie's bed and wouldn't come off – she actually had to lift the dog and take her outside to do a wee, and then she would come back indoors and head straight back to Sophie's bed again. She did that for two weeks until 5pm on the day we were due back, when Bebe got off Sophie's bed and came downstairs and sat by the back door wagging her tail – and that was the precise time that our plane landed at Heathrow. When David and I got married, Bebe was a bridesmaid. I kid you not.

Clark Kent was killed after chasing a deer. I had been out walking him and he sped off, spotted a deer and was killed by a passing car as he crossed the road, three miles from where I had been walking him. Somebody had stopped and took a note of the details from Clark Kent's collar, and then phoned me to tell me they had found his body.

It turned out that he had managed to acquire for himself a whole gaggle of human girlfriends, who came round to the house and sobbed. There was one woman he liked to watch having a bath, and he would eat her dinner if she left it on the table unattended, but she loved him.

Next we had Cassie and Chloe, who were lhasa apsos. They came to us via our dog groomer – one came from a family who were splitting up, the other's owner was dying. Then came Puppy Wuppy, a shih tzu-Yorkie cross whom I have already mentioned. I picked up the local paper and saw an advert: "Good home wanted for shih tze-Yorkie cross", and said to Sophie: "Let's go and have a look."

This tiny little animal was supposed to be Sophie's dog but she became a fixture on *Liza's Country*. She adored travelling with me and staying in hotels and suchlike, and was a great companion. I still miss her. When a dog dies you think: "Right, that's it, we are not going to have any more animals. I can't bear to go through this pain again." But it never quite works out like that, and other dogs always appear.

Just before Adelaide was born we got a Labrador called Scoter for David. Then I got Daisy, another Labrador who had been bred as a show dog, but her back was too long and her tail was too short so she had been left in a kennel in a back garden and was a real handful, and still is.

When Scoter died, we replaced him with Donald, who is just wonderful and is particularly partial to a quick chorus of: "Donald where's your troosers?"

Honey is a lhasa-Jack Russell cross, and she is my mother's dog, but obviously I now look after her. Oh yes, and I mustn't forget Kassie, who was given to me in the car park at Morrison's supermarket. I have had around 24 dogs of my own, and that is without counting the ones that I have kept for a short while before finding new homes for them.

I sometimes think that a flat in London with no animals would be great, but I would hate it.

CHAPTER 33
MY FAVOURITE THINGS

"There are still parts of the Lake District that are largely undiscovered by the mainstream holidaymakers and day trippers. You just have to know where to look."

You will know by now how important Norfolk is to me, but there are several other places that I absolutely adore, chief among those being the Lake District.

When my parents divorced, and Dad married Pam Luke, a make-up artist who worked for Yorkshire TV, she had a place in Glenridding, which is not far from Ullswater. Pam gave birth to William, three months before I had Thom, and the first time I went to visit them I had my baby with me and I just fell in love with the place.

It was 1976 and this was the first time I had ever been to the Lake District, and I just couldn't get enough of it. When I got home, I couldn't get it out of my head, so I tried to return as often as I could, and every time I went back I discovered another part of it, another hidden gem.

Some people say that the thing that spoils the Lake District is all the tourists, but back then there were hardly any. In fact, Dad had an idea to open a bed and breakfast establishment, but there simply were not enough people visiting the area to have made it a sound business proposition, so he abandoned it. All that you had then were serious hill walkers, and a lot of them brought their own tents with them and camped out in the freezing cold and wet and tried to convince themselves, and each other, that they were having a good time.

Obviously, it is all very different now – there are entire streets in places like Windermere that seem to contain nothing but hotels and guesthouses.

There are still parts of the Lake District that are largely undiscovered by the mainstream holidaymakers and day trippers. You just have to know where to look. And despite the influx of the tourists, the whole area remains largely unspoilt.

I also love Scotland, which is full of the most breathtaking scenery. We have relatives who live just outside Elgin and we often stay with them – and while we have been with them we have been lucky enough to witness the Northern Lights, which is the most beautiful natural spectacle. It really is a wondrous sight to behold, and leaves you totally transfixed.

Many of you will have seen the programme in which Joanna Lumley went off in search of the Northern Lights – although it looked spectacular on camera, it bears no comparison with seeing them for yourself. Despite all the technology at our fingertips today, a camera cannot really capture the magnitude of it all.

Of course, I also spent those years in Australia, and loved that too, but when you live somewhere you tend to take it all for granted, and it wasn't really until I returned to England that I realised how much I missed it. I also visited New Zealand, which is another extraordinary place.

And I fell in love with the Camargue region of France, which I discovered with David, who had been there to make a film about John

Skeaping, the renowned artist and sculptor. Born in 1901 in South Woodford in Essex, Skeaping studied at Goldsmith's College, London and later at the Royal Academy. He was the first husband of the sculptor Barbara Hepworth, with whom he exhibited during the 1920s. He was a member of the London Group, and later worked for a while in Mexico. He was elected to the Royal Academy in 1960. He spent some time living in Chagford in Devon and in 1959 he moved to the Camargue, where he remained until his death.

Skeaping was a colourful character who had a bull farm in the Camargue and used to spend most of his days riding around on a white horse, on which he used to round up the bulls.

For me, of course, one of the attractions of that particular part of France was the horses, which are beautiful animals. The saddles they use are incredibly comfortable, like sitting in an armchair. They are also very stable, so anybody can get on and ride, and Sophie and I loved it. We used to ride for hours.

I am a big fan or Ireland, too, and not just because I came back from there with a horse. Again, as with the Lake District and Scotland, huge parts of it are unspoilt, just as they would have been hundreds of years ago.

Holidays tend to be dictated by work, and because I usually work right through the summer we tend to go away during the winter. My birthday falls on 20 January and I have celebrated it several times in Venice – forget any images you might have about it being a smelly, overcrowded city. If you go during the winter, you will see Venice at its glorious best. Cold yes, but stunning. All the galleries and suchlike are open, and you get to see them without having to jostle for position, so you can just take your time to take it all in.

One year our trip coincided with the carnival. We had to keep diving into coffee shops for mugs of hot chocolate to keep warm, but it was a tremendous spectacle. The people spend all year making their outfits and then everybody comes out and tries to outdo their friends and neighbours. It was so colourful.

They stand on street corners and pose, and love it when tourists take their picture. Think Notting Hill Carnival with a touch more style, and you will get an idea of what the Venice Carnival is all about. It concluded with a procession into the heart of Venice, followed by a huge ball.

Mongolia is another unfulfilled ambition, and it would be special to see the horse racing that happens there – it is the second most popular sport in Mongolia, behind wrestling. They have a special meeting during the summer when all the tribes come together and have a festival of racing and play polo – in the old days, the ball used to be the head of an enemy, but I am assured they now use a proper ball, made from a yak bladder.

I would like to take part in a 'proper' walk, maybe starting out by going from coast to coast, and eventually building up to the route of the Silk Road that connects East, South and Western Asia – something that would take me several months and give me the opportunity to raise money for charity. What an adventure that would be. If Joanna Lumley can get a film crew to go with her to exotic locations, then maybe there is still a chance that I can do it too.

I had always said that I wanted to play Lady Bracknall in Oscar Wilde's *The Importance of Being Earnest* and in 1997 I finally got the chance to do so alongside Dora Brien.

I still have some ambitions within my profession, and would love to play Gertrude in *Hamlet*, but I am not sure that anybody will ever ask me now, and I long to do Mrs Malaprop in Sheridan's *The Rivals*, but

Penelope Keith did it wonderfully well not so long ago. The thing is that most of us know real-life Mrs Malaprops, people who consistently use get their words mixed up, thinking something means one thing when it actually means something else entirely.

I think it pretty astonishing that something that was written more than 220 years ago, as *The Rivals* was, remains as funny and as relevant today as it was when it was first performed. It says a great deal about the skill of Sheridan. Shakespeare's plays are also still relevant, of course, but they were different because they are almost all historical works.

You just wouldn't think that something people found funny in 1775 would still make audiences laugh today, but *The Rivals* most certainly does.

I have never been in a position where I have been able to say: "I want to do that, that and that..." and have people fall on their knees and reply: "Yes Liza, of course you can. Just leave it to me to sort it all out."

I have always had to wait to be asked, and that is the way of it with most people who work in my profession. Thanks to Bill Kenwright, I got to play the lead role In W. Somerset Maugham's *The Constant Wife*, which is an amazing part for any woman to play. It was a role I never believed I would be asked to do, and to be honest, I really didn't know the play all that well.

On the plus side, I am constantly surprised by the things that people ask me to do, that they believe I am capable of doing. I hope that by now you have some idea of what acting has meant to me, and how incredibly blessed I feel.

As for who I really am...Am I really that fluffy, dizzy blonde that I have been asked to portray so many times? No. I suppose that I would describe myself as being quite serious, which may sound odd when you know how much comedy work I have done, but maybe that is why I am drawn to it. Perhaps it is because it gives me some balance.

And the best comedy always has seriousness at its heart – it is driven by drama and by characters that audiences must believe in.

I would like to think that the people who know me would also say that I can be funny, that I am trustworthy and that I am generous. I know that sometimes I can be insensitive and that I say things and immediately wish that I hadn't. I know that I can also be intolerant at times, and get wound up by inequality and injustice.

I will rush to defend people, sometimes foolishly and without thinking about the consequences. You know the sort of thing I am talking about – everybody has said that they agree with you, that they are right behind you and will support you to the bitter end and then, just when you need them, you turn round and they have all disappeared because they have had a chance to sit down and mull over what could happen.

Loyalty is important to me, and I believe the fact that I have friends I have known for most of my life speaks for itself – and loyalty is, of course, something that has to work both ways. I care deeply for animals, and I hate to see any creature being mistreated.

My career has given me a great deal of joy. I have earned good money, enough to give me a comfortable lifestyle, but it was never quite enough to be able to tuck huge amounts away in the bank.

But am I ready to pack it all in? And if I did say: "Right, that's it. Enough is enough," what would I do if the producers of *Coronation Street* finally made that call to me? Or what if I picked up the phone one day and it was Alan Ayckbourn on the other end? "Liza, it's Alan. I've just finished another play and I want you to play the leading role. Rehearsals begin in Scarborough tomorrow. Are you interested?"

I reckon that you all know the answer. I am afraid it is in the blood, and it always will be.

Not so terribly long ago, I had the chance to return to Australia for a *Where Are They Now?* programme. Sadly, most of the original cast of *Skippy* chose not to take part, which was a great shame, but it was quite poignant to return to the spot where most of those episodes of a simple children's series were filmed.

Not a lot had changed. It was as if time had stood still and I was that 17-year-old girl again. Just for a moment, I thought that I glimpsed John and Googie sitting under a parasol as a kangaroo bounded by, a young boy's voice said: What's that Skip?", a soundman fainted and an emu was brought on set in a wheelbarrow. But it turned out to be wishful thinking.

I may owe it all to a kangaroo, but I think it all turned out rather well in the end.